White Rose MATHS

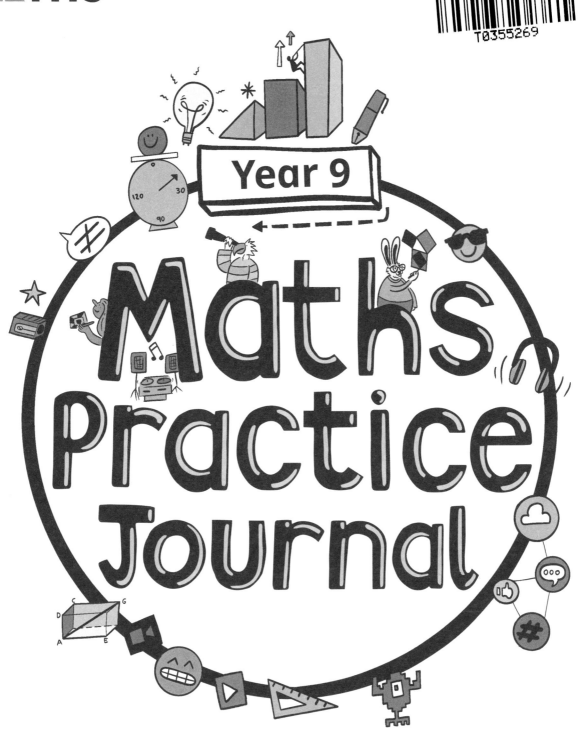

Year 9

Maths Practice Journal

Author: Ian Davies

Series Editor: MK Connolly

OXFORD

UNIVERSITY PRESS

Contents

In this block, you learn about **straight line graphs**. You use **equations** to describe the rule that links two quantities x and y. Here is an example of the type of equation that you use.

$$y = 3x + 1$$

You represent the **relationship** between x and y in a **table of values**. Here is the table for the equation $y = 3x + 1$. For every value of x, the table shows you a value of y

x	−2	−1	0	1	2
$y = 3x + 1$	−5	−2	1	4	7

You can draw and use **graphs** to represent the relationship between x and y. Here is the graph of $y = 3x + 1$. Can you see how it links to the table above?

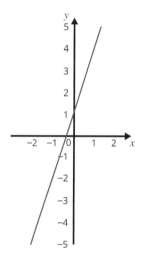

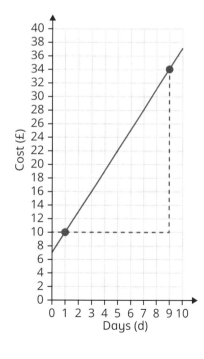

You also learn about the **gradient** of a straight line graph, and see what it means in real-life problems. This graph shows the cost of hiring a carpet cleaner.

Key vocabulary

Graph   Straight line graph   Equation   Relationship

Table of values   Gradient   Function   Linear

Straight line graphs

Date:

Let's remember

1 Circle the outlier in the data.

   5   0   83   3   1   4   2

2 Find the mean of 17, 20, 21 and 22 ☐

3 What is $\frac{1}{4}$ of 300? ☐

4 What is the sum of adjacent angles on a straight line? ☐

Let's practise

1 Lines l_1 and l_2 are shown on a coordinate grid.

   a) Write the coordinates of points A, B and C.

      A = _____   C = _____

      B = _____

   b) What is the equation of l_1? _____

   c) Write the coordinates of three points on l_2

      _____

   d) What is the equation of l_2? _____

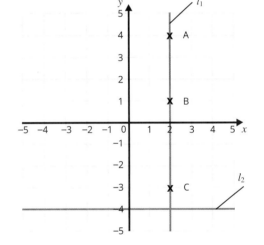

2 Here are two lines drawn on a coordinate grid.

   a) Circle the equation of l_1

      $x = 0$ $y = 0$ $y = x$ $y = -x$

   b) Circle the equation of l_2

      $x = 0$ $y = 0$ $y = x$ $y = -x$

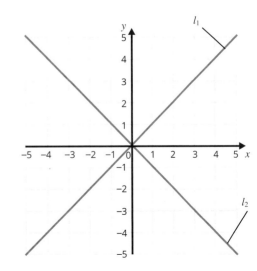

4

3   Here is a table of values for some points on the line $y = 3x + 1$

x	–2	–1	0	1	2
$y = 3x + 1$	–5	–2	1	4	

a) What is the value of y when $x = 0$? _____

b) Which of these points lie on the line $y = 3x + 1$?

   Circle your answers.

   (–2, –5)   (–5, –2)   (1, 4)   (4, 1)   (1, 3)

c) Fill in the missing value in the table.

4   Complete the table of values for the line $y = 5x - 2$

x	–2	–1	0	1	2
$y = 5x - 2$	–12			3	

5   a) Complete the table of values for the line $y = 2x + 3$

x	–2	–1	0	1	2
$y = 2x + 3$		1			

b) Use your answer to part a) to draw the graph of $y = 2x + 3$ on the grid.

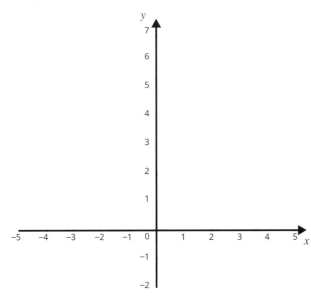

6   Four lines have been drawn on the axes.

Match the graphs to the equations.

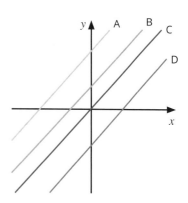

A

$y = x$

B

$y = x + 5$

C

$y = x - 3$

D

$y = x + 1$

7   Which of these straight lines have the same gradient?

Circle your answers.

$y = 3x + 2$ $y = 2x + 3$ $y = -3x + 2$ $y = 2x - 3$ $y = -2x + 3$

8   Which of these straight lines intercept the y-axis at the same point?

Circle your answers.

$y = x + 2$ $y = 3x - 2$ $y = -3x + 2$ $y = 2x - 3$ $y = -2x + 3$

9   Ron thinks the straight lines $y = 3x$ and $y = -3x$ have the same gradient.

Is Ron correct? _____

Explain your answer.

_____

_____

10   Write the equations of two lines with the same gradient as $y = 3x + 5$

_____

_____

11   a) Which of these is the equation of the y-axis?

Circle your answer.

$x = 0$ $x = y$ $y = x$ $y = 0$

b) Write the equation of the x-axis. _____

How did you find these questions?

Very easy   1   2   3   4   5   6   7   8   9   10   Very difficult

Straight line graphs

Date:

Let's remember

1   Complete the table of values for the line $y = 3x + 2$

x	–2	–1	0	1	2
$y = 3x + 2$	–4		2		

2   Work out the mean of 8, 10, 6, 8 and 9

3   What is the sum of angles around a point?

4   The radius of a circle is 6 cm.

   What is the length of the diameter?   cm

Let's practise

1   Circle the equations whose lines have a gradient of 3

   $y = 2x + 3$ $y = 3x + 2$ $y = \frac{1}{3}x - 2$ $y = 5 - 3x$

2   Complete the table.

Equation of line	Gradient of line	Coordinates of y-intercept
$y = 5x + 1$	5	
$y = 3x + 2$		(0, 2)
$y = 4x - 1$		
	3	(0, 4)
	2	(0, –5)
	–2	(0, 7)
$y = -3x - 4$		

3 Here is a straight line graph.

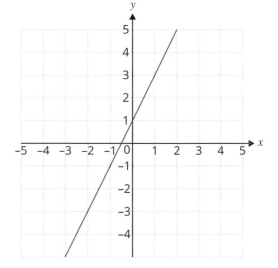

a) Work out the gradient of the line.

b) Write the coordinates of the point where the line meets the y-axis. _____

c) Complete the equation of the line.

$y = \boxed{}\, x + \boxed{}$

4 Write the equations in the form $y = mx + c$

a) $3y = 6x + 12$ _____

b) $\frac{y}{2} = x - 3$ _____

c) $2y = 10 + 6x$ _____

5 The graph shows the cost, £C, of hiring a carpet cleaner for d days.

a) Work out the gradient of the line.

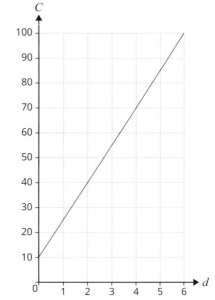

b) What does the gradient represent?

_____

c) Write the equation of the line.

_____

6 A team of 3 people can paint a house in 12 hours.

How long would it take a team of 9 people working at the same rate to paint the house?

$\boxed{}$ hours

7   Some groups are each given 24 sweets.
    Each group shares the sweets equally.

a) Complete the table.

Number of people in the group	Number of sweets each person gets
1	24
2	12
3	
4	
6	
8	
12	

b) Show this information as a graph on
   the axes.

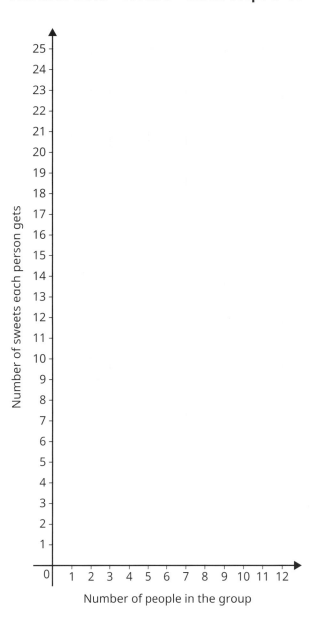

8   a) What is the gradient of a straight line that is perpendicular to a straight line
       with gradient $\frac{1}{5}$? [   ]

    b) What is the gradient of a straight line that is perpendicular to a straight line
       with gradient −4? [   ]

How did you find these questions?

Very easy   1   2   3   4   5   6   7   8   9   10   Very difficult

Block 2 Forming & solving equations

In this block, you build on your knowledge of **equations** from last year. Here is an example of the type of equation that you **solve**. That means you find the value of x

$$4x + 7 = 43$$

You can use a **bar model** to help solve harder equations like this one.

$$4x + 12 = 2x + 30$$

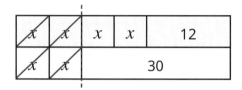

You also solve **inequalities**. That is where there is an inequality sign instead of an equals sign. This one means the answer to something multiplied by 2, then add 9, is greater than 15. Can you work out what range of values w could take?

$$2w + 9 > 15$$

You also use **function machines** to help you understand **formulae**. Can you write a formula for this function machine?

input ⟶ × 3 ⟶ − 8 ⟶ output

Key vocabulary

Equation   Inequality   Greater than   Less than   Solve   Solution

Unknown   Formulae   Bar model   Function machine

Forming & solving equations

Date:

Let's remember

1 What is the gradient of the line $y = 3x + 4$? _____

2 Complete the table of values for $y = 3x - 1$

x	-2	-1	0	1	2
$y = 3x - 1$	-7		-1		

3 Work out the range of the data.

10   12   8   11   76   8   11

4 How many lines of symmetry does a rectangle have?

Let's practise

1 Solve the equations.

a) $x + 7 = 23$

b) $5p = 20$

c) $\frac{q}{5} = 12$

$x = $ ☐

$p = $ ☐

$q = $ ☐

2 Solve the inequalities.

a) $m - 8 > 12$

b) $n + 5 < 18$

c) $\frac{t}{2} \leq 80$

_____   _____   _____

3 Solve the equations.

a) $4a + 7 = 43$ 　　　　 b) $4a - 7 = 43$ 　　　　 c) $\dfrac{a}{4} + 7 = 43$

$a = \boxed{}$ 　　　　 $a = \boxed{}$ 　　　　 $a = \boxed{}$

4 Solve $5(x + 3) = 100$

$x = \boxed{}$

5 a) Explain why the equations $6(p - 2) = 66$ and $66 = 6(p - 2)$ have the same solution.

_____

_____

b) Solve $66 = 6(p - 2)$

$p = \boxed{}$

6 Solve the inequalities.

a) $2w + 9 > 15$ 　　　　 b) $\dfrac{x + 5}{2} \leq 8$ 　　　　 c) $3 > 2y + 1$

_____ 　　　　 _____ 　　　　 _____

7 Circle the numbers that satisfy the inequality $5 - x > 2$

2 　　 5 　　 −1 　　 0 　　 4 　　 3

8   Here is Mo's solution to the inequality $10 - 2x < 3$

$$10 - 2x \quad < 3$$
$$-10 \qquad -10$$
$$2x < -7$$
$$\div 2 \quad \div 2$$
$$x < -3.5$$

a) Explain Mo's mistake.

_____

b) Find the correct solution to $10 - 2x < 3$

_____

9   Eva has drawn a bar model to solve $4x + 12 = 2x + 30$

Complete Eva's working.

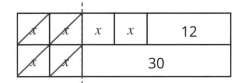

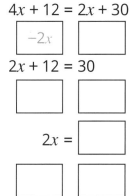

$4x + 12 = 2x + 30$

$-2x$ ☐

$2x + 12 = 30$

☐ ☐

$2x =$ ☐

☐ ☐

$x =$ ☐

10   Solve the equations.

a) $3a + 16 = 5a + 2$

$a =$ ☐

b) $6p + 7 = 2p + 3$

$p =$ ☐

c) $5g - 3 = 2g + 3$

$c =$ ☐

d) $w - 4 = 6w - 29$

$w =$ ☐

11   Solve the inequalities.

a) $6t + 4 > 3t + 22$

b) $2b - 10 < 4b - 4$

_____   _____

How did you find these questions?

Very easy   1   2   3   4   5   6   7   8   9   10   Very difficult

Forming & solving equations

Date:

Let's remember

1   Solve $p + 12 = 37$

$p = $ ⬚

2   What is the gradient of the line $y = 4x$? ⬚

3   Find the median of 6, 19, 7, 12 and 9 ⬚

4   Calculate the area of the trapezium. ⬚ cm²

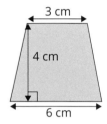

3 cm

4 cm

6 cm

Let's practise

1   The perimeter of this triangle is 30 cm.

a) Show that $6x = 30$

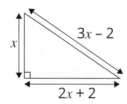

$3x - 2$

x

$2x + 2$

b) Work out the length of each side of the triangle.

$x = $ ⬚ cm $2x + 2 = $ ⬚ cm $3x - 2 = $ ⬚ cm

2   The perimeter of this rectangle is 54 cm.

a) Form and solve an equation to work out the value of x

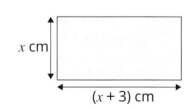

x cm

$(x + 3)$ cm

_____

$x = $ ⬚

b) Work out the area of the rectangle. ⬚ cm²

3   Annie thinks of a number, n

She halves her number and adds 5

The answer is greater than 12

Form and solve an inequality to work out the smallest integer that Annie could be thinking of.

_____

4   Tick the cards that show formulae.

$A = lw$ πd $S = \frac{D}{T}$ $2d + 3 = 20$ $V = \pi r^2 h$

5   $P = 2a + 2b$ is a formula for the perimeter of a rectangle with side lengths a and b.

a) Work out the value of P when $a = 8$ and $b = 6$

$P =$ ☐

b) Work out the value of a when $P = 40$ and $b = 7$

$a =$ ☐

6   $F = ma$ is a formula used in maths and physics.

a) Work out the value of F when $m = 40$ and $a = 1.5$

$F =$ ☐

b) Work out the value of a when $F = 60$ and $m = 120$

$a =$ ☐

c) Work out the value of m when $F = 14$ and $a = 0.7$

$m =$ ☐

7   Rearrange the formulae to make x the subject.

a) $p = x + 6$ b) $t = 10 - x$ c) $g = \frac{x}{5}$

_____   _____   _____

8   The formula for the circumference, C, of a circle of diameter d is $C = \pi d$

Find the formula for the diameter, d, of a circle of circumference C

_____

9   Here is a function machine.

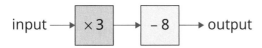

a) Work out the output when the input is 10

b) Work out the input when the output is 10

c) Circle the formula to find the output b from the input a

$a = 3b - 8$ $b = 3a - 8$ $a = 3(b - 8)$ $b = 3(a - 8)$

10   Rearrange the formulae to make t the subject.

a) $a = 3t + 6$ b) $b = \dfrac{t - y}{5}$

_____   _____

11   Rearrange the formulae to make d the subject.

a) $M = 3d^2 - q$ b) $t = 3(p + \sqrt{d})$

_____   _____

How did you find these questions?

Very easy   1   2   3   4   5   6   7   8   9   10   Very difficult

Block 3 Testing conjectures

In this block, you learn about **conjectures**. This means you use a lot of **reasoning**. Firstly, there is a reminder about factors, multiples and prime numbers. Do you know which of these cards show multiples of 3?

20	21	22	23	24	25	26	27	28	29

You work out whether **conjectures** are **true** or **false**. Do you think this conjecture is true or false?

The difference between two odd numbers is odd.

You also write algebraic expressions from word descriptions. However, you need to be careful and remember to use the correct order of operations. Here is an example: below are two expressions. Which expression matches '3 less than 5 multiplied by n'?

Can you see why the expression on the left is correct and the one on the right is wrong?

$5n - 3$	$2n$

You also look for patterns in hundred squares. Here is part of a hundred square with a U shape shaded in. Can you see any patterns between the numbers in the U?

What if the U was in a different place in the hundred square?

1	2	3	4	5	6	7	8	9	10
11	12	13	14	15	16	17	18	19	20
21	22	23	24	25	26	27	28	29	30
31	32	33	34	35	36	37	38	39	40
41	42	43	44	45	46	47	48	49	50
51	52	53	54	55	56	57	58	59	60

Key vocabulary

Conjecture   True False   Show that   Explain

Factor   Prime   Multiple   Expression

Testing conjectures

Date:

Let's remember

1 Solve $5a + 1 = 2a + 10$

$a = \boxed{}$

2 Solve $3x + 1 > 16$ _____

3 Circle the equations of lines that are parallel to the x-axis.

$x = 5$ $y = 5$ $y = x$ $x = -5$ $y = -5$

4 Write the sum of the exterior angles of a triangle. $\boxed{}$

Let's practise

1 a) List all the factors of 15 _____

   b) List the first five multiples of 15 _____

2 Here are some number cards.

| 20 | 21 | 22 | 23 | 24 | 25 | 26 | 27 | 28 | 29 |

   a) Which of the cards are prime numbers? _____

   b) Which of the cards are multiples of 4? _____

   c) Which of the cards are factors of 100? _____

3 Are the statements true or false?

   a) 1 is a factor of all whole numbers. _____

   b) The angles of an isosceles triangle add up to 180° _____

   c) 12 is a multiple of 12 _____

   d) $\frac{1}{3} + \frac{2}{5} = \frac{3}{8}$ _____

   e) $\frac{1}{3} \times \frac{2}{5} = \frac{2}{15}$ _____

4   Dexter says:

"It will either snow tomorrow or it won't, so the probability of snow tomorrow is

one half."

Is Dexter's statement true or false? _____

Explain your answer.

_____

_____

5   Give an example of when the statements are true and when they are false.

Statement	Example when true	Example when false
Factors of 16 are even		
Multiples of 5 end in a 5		
Multiples of 7 are odd		
Odd numbers are prime		

6   Decide if the statements are always, sometimes or never true.

Circle your answers.

a) A list of numbers has a mean.

   Always true   Sometimes true   Never true

b) A list of numbers has a median.

   Always true   Sometimes true   Never true

c) A list of numbers has a mode.

   Always true   Sometimes true   Never true

d) The difference between two odd numbers is odd.

   Always true   Sometimes true   Never true

7   Is each algebraic statement always, sometimes or never true?

a) If n is even, $\frac{n}{2}$ is odd. _____

b) $2x + 1 = 100$ _____

c) $x + 12 > x + 21$ _____

8 Here is a triangle.

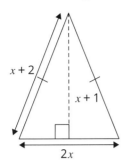

a) Show that the perimeter of the triangle is $4x + 4$

_____

_____

b) Show that the area of the triangle is $x^2 + x$

_____

_____

_____

9 Show that 30% of 50 = 50% of 30

_____

_____

10 Show that $6(x + 4) + 4(2x + 6) \equiv 2(7x + 24)$

_____

_____

11 a) Is the conjecture true? _____

> The difference between an odd number and an even number is even.

Explain your answer.

_____

b) Make a conjecture about the difference between two even numbers.

_____

How did you find these questions?

Very easy   1   2   3   4   5   6   7   8   9   10   Very difficult

Testing conjectures

Date:

Let's remember

1 Write all the factors of 20 _____

2 Use the formula $F = ma$ to work out F when $m = 60$ and $a = 1.5$

$F =$ ☐

3 A straight line has gradient −2 and intercepts the y-axis at (0, 4).

Circle the correct equation of the line.

$y = 2x + 4$ $y = 2x - 4$ $y = -2x - 4$ $y = -2x + 4$

4 Work out the range of 8, 12, 7, 16, 20 and 9 ☐

Let's practise

1 a) Simplify the terms.

i) $4 \times x$ ii) $x \times 4$ iii) $x \times x$ iv) $-3 \times x$

_____   _____   _____   _____

b) Simplify the expressions.

i) $3x + 5x$ ii) $5x - 3x$ iii) $3x - 5x$ iv) $-5x - 3x$

_____   _____   _____   _____

2 Expand the brackets.

a) $4(x + 2)$ b) $6(x + 3)$ c) $5(x - 1)$ d) $x(x + 2)$

_____   _____   _____   _____

3 a) Expand the brackets.

i) $x(x + 4)$ _____

ii) $5(x + 4)$ _____

b) Use your answers to part a) to expand and simplify $(x + 5)(x + 4)$

_____

_____

4   Expand and simplify.

a) $(x + 3)(x + 6)$

_____

_____

b) $(y + 2)(y + 5)$

_____

_____

c) $(w + 7)(w + 1)$

_____

_____

d) $(a + 4)(a + 4)$

_____

_____

e) $(t + 4)(t - 1)$

_____

_____

f) $(p + 3)(p - 4)$

_____

_____

g) $(s - 2)(s + 6)$

_____

_____

h) $(h + 5)(h - 5)$

_____

_____

5   Write an algebraic expression to represent each statement.

a) 5 more than m _____

b) 5 less than m _____

c) 5 multiplied by m _____

d) 2 more than 5 multiplied by m _____

6   Given that n is a positive integer, complete the statements.

a) $3n$ is a multiple of _____

b) $2n$ is an _____ number

c) _____ n is a multiple of 10

d) If n is odd, then $n + 1$ is _____

7   Dani says, "All the terms in the sequence given by the rule $6n + 2$ are even."

Decide if Dani is correct and explain your answer.

_____

_____

_____

8   Here is part of a hundred square.

The highlighted block is called U_{12}

The value of the block is the total of the numbers inside the block.

So, the value of U_{12} is:

12 + 22 + 32 + 33 + 34 + 24 + 14 = 171

1	2	3	4	5	6	7	8	9	10
11	12	13	14	15	16	17	18	19	20
21	22	23	24	25	26	27	28	29	30
31	32	33	34	35	36	37	38	39	40
41	42	43	44	45	46	47	48	49	50
51	52	53	54	55	56	57	58	59	60

a) Draw the blocks U_5 and U_{38} on the hundred square and work out their values.

$U_5 =$ _____ $U_{38} =$ _____

b) Complete the table showing U_x

x		$x + 2$
$x + 10$		$x + 12$

c) Write a simplified expression for the value of U_x _____

d) Use your answer to part c) to work out the value of U_{75} [ ]

9   a) Expand and simplify $(x + 3)(x + 4)$

_____

_____

b) Use your answer to a) to help expand and simplify $(x + 3)(x + 4)(x + 5)$

_____

_____

_____

How did you find these questions?

Very easy   1   2   3   4   5   6   7   8   9   10   Very difficult

Block 4 Three-dimensional shapes

In this block, you learn about **three-dimensional shapes**. That includes **cuboids** and **cones** that you have seen before.

Can you name this **3-D** shape? Here is a clue – it starts with T.

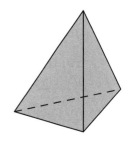

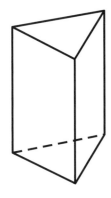

You explore **prisms**. This one has 9 **edges**. Can you work out how many **vertices** and **faces** it has?

You also sketch and recognise **nets** of shapes. Here is a net for the prism above. Do you know what kind of prism it is?

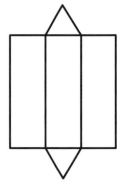

You also work with **plans** and **elevations.** Here are some examples.

Can you sketch the 3-D shape that they represent?

Plan	Front	Side
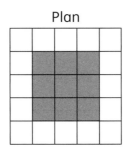	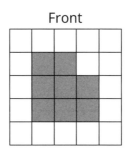	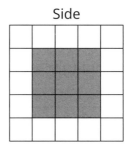

Key vocabulary

Three-dimensional (3-D)   Prism   Cuboid   Cone

Pyramid   Cylinder   Tetrahedron   Edge   Vertex   Face

Plan   Elevation   Net   Surface area

Three-dimensional shapes

Date:

Let's remember

1 Expand and simplify $(x + 3)(x + 7)$

_____

_____

2 Show that the statement is false.

All multiples of 9 are odd.

_____

_____

3 Solve $3x + 5 > 2$

_____

4 How many lines of symmetry does an equilateral triangle have? ☐

Let's practise

1 Write the mathematical name of each 2-D shape.

a)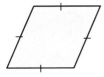

_____

c)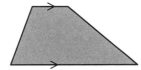

_____

e)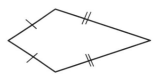

_____

b)

_____

d)

_____

f)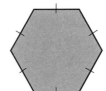

_____

2 Write the mathematical name of each 3-D shape.

a)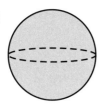

_____

c)

_____

b)

_____

d)

_____

3 Decide if the statements are true or false.

a) A triangle can be right-angled and isosceles.   _____

b) A trapezium cannot have a line of symmetry.   _____

c) A parallelogram has 4 equal sides.   _____

d) A cuboid has 13 faces.   _____

4 Tick the shapes that are prisms.

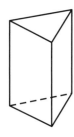 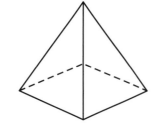  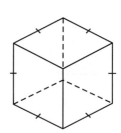

5 Complete the table.

Shape	Number of edges	Number of vertices	Number of faces
Cuboid			
Tetrahedron			
Triangular prism			

6   Tick the nets that would make a cube.

7   Draw an accurate net for the cuboid shown.

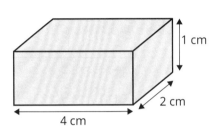

1 cm

2 cm

4 cm

8   Which 3-D shapes can made from these nets?

a)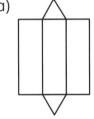

b)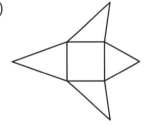

_____   _____

9   Sketch the net of a hexagonal-based pyramid.

How did you find these questions?

Very easy   1   2   3   4   5   6   7   8   9   10   Very difficult

27

Three-dimensional shapes

Date:

Let's remember

1   What is the mathematical name for a shape with 4 equal sides and 4 equal angles?

_____

2   Expand and simplify $(x + 1)(x + 4)$

_____

_____

3   Use the formula $p = q + r$ to work out the value of p when $q = 17$ and $r = 96$

$p =$ [   ]

4   What do the angles in a triangle add up to?   [   ]

Let's practise

1   Here is a cuboid.

On the grid, draw the plan, the front elevation and side elevations of the cuboid.

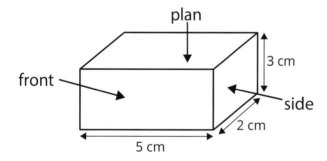

2   Here is a shape made from interlocking cubes.

   On the grid, draw the plan, the front elevation
   and side elevation of the shape.

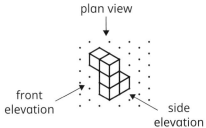

plan view

front
elevation

side
elevation

3   Work out the area of each shape.

a)

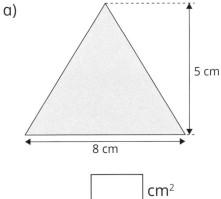

5 cm

8 cm

[ ] cm²

b)

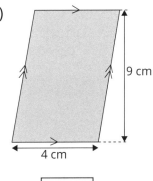

9 cm

4 cm

[ ] cm²

c)

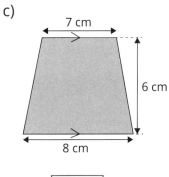

7 cm

6 cm

8 cm

[ ] cm²

4   The edges of a cube are 8 cm long.
   Work out the surface area of the cube. [ ] cm²

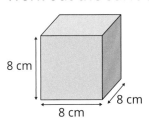

8 cm

8 cm

8 cm

5   Work out the surface area of the cuboid. [ ] cm²

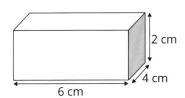

2 cm

4 cm

6 cm

6   Work out the surface area of the triangular prism.

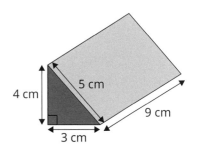

surface area = ⬚ cm²

7   Work out the surface area of the cylinder.

Give your answer to the nearest whole number.

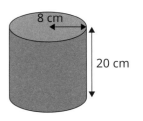

surface area = ⬚ cm²

8   The width of a cuboid is x cm.

The height of a cuboid is double its width.

The length of the cuboid is double its height.

Work out an expression for the surface area of the cuboid.

surface area = ⬚ cm²

9   Here are a cuboid and a triangular prism.

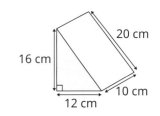

The cuboid and the triangular prism have the same surface area.

Work out the value of h

h = ⬚ cm

How did you find these questions?

Very easy   1   2   3   4   5   6   7   8   9   10   Very difficult

30

Three-dimensional shapes

Date:

Let's remember

1. Find the surface area of a cube with sides of length 5 cm. [   ] cm²

2. Tick the shapes that are prisms.

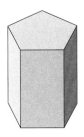   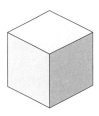 

3. Work out $\frac{2}{3}$ of 60 [   ]

4. Work out the sum of the interior angles of an octagon. [   ]

Let's practise

1. A cube has a side length of 20 cm.

   Work out the volume of the cube. [   ] cm³

2. Work out the volume of the cuboid.

   Give units with your answer.

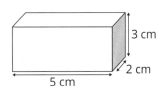

   Volume = _____

3 The cuboid ABCDEFGH is split to

   form two identical cubes.

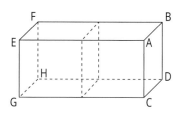

   AB = 10 cm

   Work out the volume of ABCDEFGH.

   volume of ABCDEFGH = ☐ cm³

4 The volume of a cube is 1000 cm³

   Work out the surface area of the cube. ☐ cm²

5 The volume of each of these cuboids is 300 cm³

   Work out the values of x and y

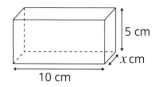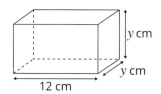

$x =$ ☐ $y =$ ☐

6 The diagram shows a water tank.

   The tank is full of water.

   How many buckets that hold 12 litres of
   water can be filled from the water tank?

   (1 litre = 1000 cm³)

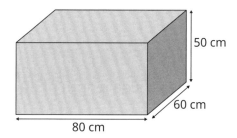

   number of buckets = ☐

7 Here is a triangular prism.

   The cross-section of the prism is a right-angled triangle.

   Calculate the volume of the prism.

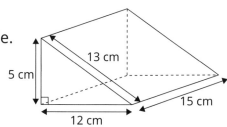

   volume = ☐ cm³

8   Work out the volume of the triangular prism.

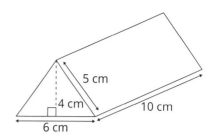

5 cm

4 cm

10 cm

6 cm

volume = [   ] cm³

9   A cylindrical tank has base radius 2 m and height 5 m.

Calculate the volume of the tank. Give your answer to 3 significant figures.

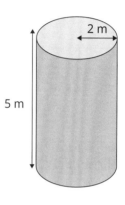

2 m

5 m

volume = [   ] m³

10 The sphere and the cone have equal volumes.

H

The radius of the sphere is 5.2 cm.

The height of the cone is 11 cm.

Work out the radius of the base of the cone.

Give your answer to 3 significant figures.

The volume of a sphere = $\frac{4}{3}\pi r^3$

The volume of a cone = $\frac{1}{3}\pi r^2 h$

radius of the base of the cone = [   ] cm

How did you find these questions?

Very easy   1   2   3   4   5   6   7   8   9   10   Very difficult

In this block, you build on the work you did on **constructions** in a previous year, but extend it to using **compasses** like these. You also explore **congruency**.

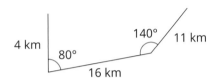

You construct and interpret **scale drawings**. This sketch shows part of a cycle route, and you can represent it accurately by drawing it to a **scale** of 1 cm to 2 km.

You also construct a **locus**, which is a set of points that follow a rule. This locus represents all points that are a fixed distance away from the **line segment**.

You also identify **congruent** shapes. Can you match up the congruent shapes on this grid?

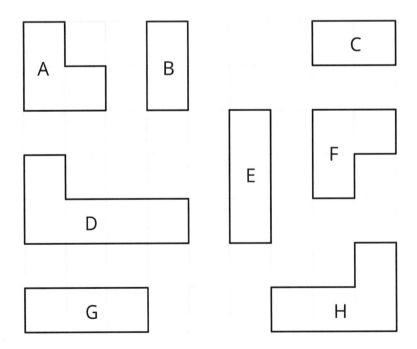

Key vocabulary

Construction   Compasses   Scale drawing   Scale   Congruence   Locus

Line segment   Perpendicular bisector   Angle bisector

Constructions & congruency

Date:

Let's remember

1   Work out the volume of a cube with side length 10 cm. ⬚ cm³

2   Work out the surface area of a cube with side length 10 cm. ⬚ cm²

3   Expand and simplify $(y + 5)(y - 1)$

_____

_____

4   Find the mean of 12, 10, 6, 1 and 7 ⬚

Let's practise

1   a) Draw an angle of 35° at point A.

•———————————
A

b) Draw an angle of 155° at point B.

•———————————
B

2   The sketch shows part of a cycle route.

Use a scale of 1 cm to 2 km to draw an accurate scale diagram of the part of the route.

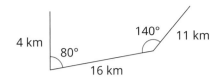

3   Choose the correct word to complete the sentence.

| straight line | ellipse | circle | square |

The locus of points the same distance from a given point is a _____

4   Use ruler and compasses in the questions below.

Draw the locus of all the points 1.5 cm from the point O.

●
O

5   Shade the set of points that are within 4 cm of P and within 3 cm of Q.

_____
P   Q

6   Draw the locus of all points that are 3 cm away from the line segment.

7   Draw the locus of all points that are the same distance from A and B.

A ✕   ✕ B

8   Construct the perpendicular bisectors of the line segments.

a)   b)

How did you find these questions?

Very easy   1   2   3   4   5   6   7   8   9   10   Very difficult

Constructions & congruency

Date:

Let's remember

1   What shape is the locus of all points that are the same distance away from a point?

_____

2   The area of the cross-section of a prism is 12 cm²

The length of the prism is 8 cm.

What is the volume of the prism? [   ] cm³

3   Work out the surface area of a cube with side length 4 cm. [   ] cm²

4   A quadrilateral has two different pairs of equal sides and four right angles.

Write the mathematical name of the shape.

_____

Let's practise

1   In each diagram, use ruler and compasses to construct the perpendicular from point C to the line segment AB.

a)   ✗ C

A ——————————————— B

b)   ✗ C

c) A  B

2 In each diagram, use ruler and compasses to construct the perpendicular to the line segment AB, which passes through the point C.

a)

b)

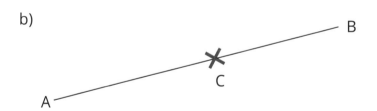

3 Show the set of points that are the same distance from AB and AC.

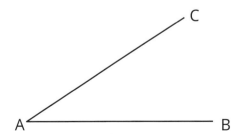

4   Use a ruler and pair of compasses to construct the angle bisector of each angle.

a)

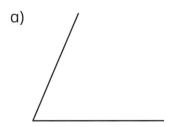

b)

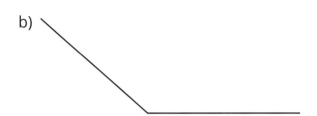

5   Shade the set of points that are closer to AB than AD **and** closer to BC than AB.

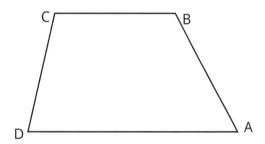

6   Here is a rectangle PQRS.

Shade the set of points that are closer to PQ than PS **and** more than 2 cm from Q.

How did you find these questions?

Very easy   1   2   3   4   5   6   7   8   9   10   Very difficult

Constructions & congruency

Date:

Let's remember

1. What does it mean to bisect an angle?

   _____

2. A scale diagram is drawn such that 1 cm represents 5 m.

   What length does 4 cm on the diagram represent? ☐ m

3. Expand and simplify $(t + 4)(t - 3)$

   _____

   _____

4. Calculate the area of a circle with radius 10 cm.

   Give your answer in terms of π

   area = _____

Let's practise

1. Make an accurate drawing of each triangle.

   a)

   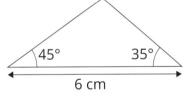

   b)

   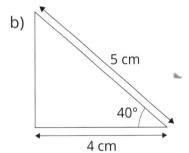

2   Use a pair of compasses to construct triangle ABC where AB = 7 cm, AC = 6 cm and BC = 5 cm.

3   Identify the pairs of congruent shapes shown on the grid.

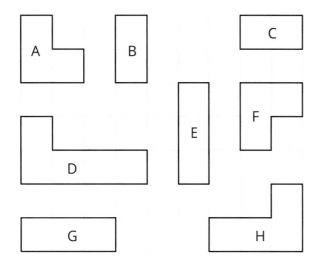

_____

4   On the grid, complete the shape on the right so it is congruent to shape A.

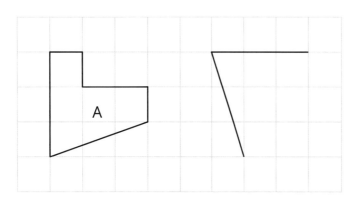

5   On the grid, draw two shapes, in different orientations, that are congruent to shape X.

6   The diagram shows two congruent triangles, ABD and BCD.

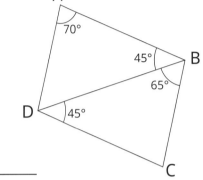

   a) Which side of ABD is equal in length to BC?

   b) Which side of BCD is equal in length to AB?

   c) What is the mathematical name of the shape ABCD?

   _____

7   Eva and Whitney both construct a triangle with angles 90°, 50° and 40°

   Eva says, "Our triangles must be congruent."

   Explain why Eva is wrong.

   _____

   _____

8   The diagram shows the diagonals of rectangle PQRS meeting at T.

   Find three pairs of congruent triangles in the diagram.

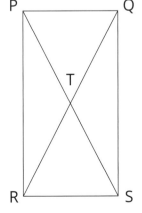

   _____

   _____

   _____

How did you find these questions?

Very easy   1   2   3   4   5   6   7   8   9   10   Very difficult

Time to reflect

Look back through the work you have done this term. Think about what you enjoyed and what you found easy or hard. Talk about this to your teacher and someone at home.

Try these questions	How do you feel about this topic? Tick the box.
Match the graphs to the equations. $$y = x - 1$$ $$y = x + 2$$ $$y = 2x + 1$$ $$y = x$$ If you need a reminder, look back at straight line graphs on pages 4–9	☐ I am confident and could teach someone else. ☐ I think I understand but I need practice. ☐ I don't understand and need help.
Use the bar model to help solve the equation $5x + 4 = 2x + 10$ $x =$ ☐ If you need a reminder, look back at equations on pages 11–16	☐ I am confident and could teach someone else. ☐ I think I understand but I need practice. ☐ I don't understand and need help.
Work out the surface area of the cuboid. surface area = ☐ cm^2 If you need a reminder, look back 3-D shapes on pages 25–33	☐ I am confident and could teach someone else. ☐ I think I understand but I need practice. ☐ I don't understand and need help.

Block 1 Numbers

In this block, you build on your understanding of number to include different types of numbers. Firstly, a reminder of what an **integer** is. Can you spot which two of these numbers are integers?

7	3.5	−2	$\frac{1}{4}$	2π	3.891

You explore **rational numbers** and **real numbers**. Here are some numbers. They are all real numbers, but √5 isn't rational.

3	√5	1.752	$\frac{3}{5}$	−5

You also review arithmetic with fractions. The answer to this calculation is $\frac{2}{3}$. Can you work it out?

$$2\frac{1}{6} \div 3\frac{1}{4}$$

You also solve real-life problems with numbers. Here is an example.

A box contains 300 beads.

$\frac{2}{5}$ of the beads are red.

$\frac{3}{4}$ of the remaining beads are white and the rest of the beads are blue.

How many more red beads are there than blue beads?

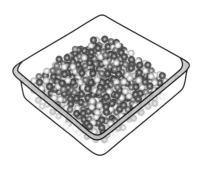

Key vocabulary

Integer   Real   Rational   Irrational   Root

Surd   LCM   HCF   Standard form

Numbers

Date:

Let's remember

1 Are the two triangles congruent? _____

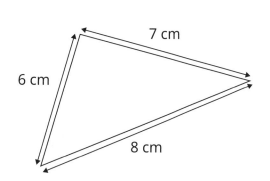
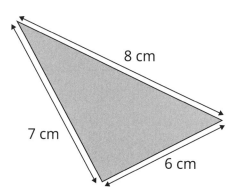

2 Is an angle of 73° acute or obtuse? _____

3 How many faces does a cuboid have? ☐

4 What is the gradient of the line $y = 7x - 9$? ☐

Let's practise

1 Here is a list of numbers.

    8   4.5   −3 $\frac{3}{4}$ π   5.172

a) Which of the numbers are integers? _____

b) Which of the numbers are rational but not integers? _____

c) Which of the numbers are not rational? _____

2 Work out the calculations.

a) −5 + 3 = ☐   c) 5 + −3 = ☐

b) −5 − 3 = ☐   d) −5 + −3 = ☐

3 Work out the calculations.

a) −5 × 3 = ☐   b) 5 × −3 = ☐   c) −5 × −3 = ☐

4   Work out the calculations.

   a) $-10 \div 2 =$ ☐

   b) $-10 \div -2 =$ ☐

   c) $10 \div -2 =$ ☐

5   Find the difference between $(-4)^2$ and -4^2 ☐

6   Mo buys 24 packs of biscuits that cost 78p each.

   How much change will Mo get from £20?

   change = £ ☐

7   It costs a factory 38p for every item they produce.

   a) How much does it cost to produce 173 items?

   £ ☐

   b) How many items would be produced for a cost of £60.80? ☐

8   Some fencing is arranged to form a regular hexagon with sides 8.7 m long.

   The fencing is rearranged to form a square.
   Work out the length of one side of the square. ☐ m

9   a) It costs £9.48 per hour to attend the local gym.

How much does it cost to go for 8 hours? £ ☐

b) It costs £58.38 to attend an event for 6 hours.

How much does it cost per hour?   £ ☐

10 A piece of card has a mass of 160 g per square metre.

Work out the mass of 0.35 m² of the card. ☐ g

11 Which of these numbers are surds?

Circle your answers.

H

$\sqrt{2}$ $\sqrt{16}$ $\sqrt{10}$ $\sqrt{12}$ $\sqrt{8}$ $\sqrt[3]{8}$

12 a) Write these calculations as single surds.

H

i) $\sqrt{7} \times \sqrt{6} =$ ☐   iii) $\sqrt{30} \div \sqrt{5} =$ ☐

ii) $\sqrt{8} \times \sqrt{5} =$ ☐   iv) $\sqrt{70} \div \sqrt{7} =$ ☐

b) Write these surds in the form $a\sqrt{b}$, where a and b are integers.

i) $\sqrt{48} =$ _____   ii) $\sqrt{175} =$ _____

How did you find these questions?

Very easy   1   2   3   4   5   6   7   8   9   10   Very difficult

Numbers

Date:

Let's remember

1   −4 × −5 = ☐

2   BC = 8 cm

Label this on the diagram.

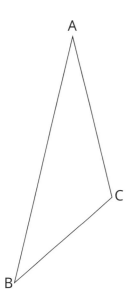

3   Is an angle of 125° acute or obtuse? _____

4   Use the formula $C = 90m + 200$ to work out the value of C when $m = 12$

$C =$ ☐

Let's practise

1   What is the highest common factor (HCF) of 40 and 48? ☐

2   What is the lowest common multiple (LCM) of 12 and 16? ☐

3   Tommy and Amir cycle around a cycle track.

Tommy takes 40 seconds to cycle each lap and Amir takes 50 seconds to cycle each lap.

They start cycling at the same time from the start line.

How many laps does each person complete before they meet at the start line again?

4   Work out the calculations.

Give your answers in their simplest form.

a) $\frac{3}{4} + \frac{1}{12} = \boxed{}$

b) $\frac{11}{12} - \frac{2}{3} = \boxed{}$

5   Work out $5\frac{3}{4} + 2\frac{3}{5}$

Give your answer as a mixed number in its simplest form.

6   Work out the calculations.

Give your answers in their simplest form.

a) $\frac{3}{4} \times \frac{5}{6} = \boxed{}$

b) $\frac{3}{4} \div \frac{5}{6} = \boxed{}$

7   Work out $2\frac{4}{5} \div 3\frac{1}{2}$

Give your answer in its simplest form. $\boxed{}$

8   A box contains 300 beads.

$\frac{2}{5}$ of the beads are red.

$\frac{3}{4}$ of the remaining beads are white and the rest of the beads are blue.

How many more red beads are there than blue beads?

9   a) Write the numbers in standard form.

   i) 840 000 = _____   ii) 0.0032 = _____

   b) Write the standard form numbers as ordinary numbers.

   i) 5.01×10^6 = _____   ii) 6.8×10^{-2} _____

10   Solve the equations.

   Give your answers in standard form.

   a) $\frac{x}{3 \times 10^{-2}} = 5 \times 10^4$ b) $y - 3 \times 10^6 = 4.8 \times 10^7$

   x = _____ y = _____

11   The capacity of Wembley stadium is 90 000

   The population of England would fill Wembley stadium 672 times.

   Work out the population of England, giving your answer in standard form.

   population of England = _____

How did you find these questions?

Very easy   1   2   3   4   5   6   7   8   9   10   Very difficult

51

Block 2   Using percentages

In this block, you build on your knowledge of **percentages**, starting by reminding yourselves of what you have already learned. Which one of these isn't equivalent to any of the others?

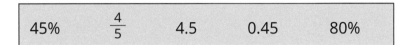

| 45% | $\frac{4}{5}$ | 4.5 | 0.45 | 80% |

You learn how to work out **reverse percentages**. That is where you know the value of something now after a percentage change, but you have to work out what it used to be. You could use a bar model to help you with this example.

Dani buys a ticket for a concert for £36

The price of the ticket had been reduced by 20%

How much did the ticket originally cost?

£36

You also work out what one number is as a percentage of another number. This is really useful, for example in working out a maths test score as a percentage.

Score 18/20

You also look at **repeated percentage change**. For example, when you increase something by 3% and then increase it by 3% again. You learn how to identify the correct multiplier to use. Only one of these is the correct multiplier for repeatedly increasing something by 3%.

| $\times 1.3^2$ | $\times 1.6$ | $\times 1.06$ | $\times 1.03^2$ |

Key vocabulary

Fraction   Decimal   Percentage   Multiplier

Increase   Decrease   Reverse   Bar model   Repeated

Using percentages

Date:

Let's remember

1   $6 \div \frac{2}{3} = \boxed{}$

2   $9 + -5 = \boxed{}$

3   The side length of a cube is 14 cm.

What is the surface area of the cube? $\boxed{}$ cm^2

4   Solve $x - 9 > 2$ _____

Let's practise

1   Match the equivalent decimals and percentages.

30%		0.03
35%		0.3
3%		0.33
33%		0.35

2   Use the fact that $\frac{1}{4}$ = 25% to convert the fractions to percentages.

a) $\frac{3}{4} = \boxed{}$

b) $\frac{1}{8} = \boxed{}$

c) $\frac{5}{8} = \boxed{}$

3   Explain how you know that $\frac{2}{3}$ is not equivalent to 23%

_____

_____

4   A bicycle costs £760

The price of the bicycle is reduced by 35% in a sale.

a) By how much is the price of the bicycle reduced?   £ ⬚

b) Work out the sale price of the bicycle.   £ ⬚

5   The population of a town in 2023 is 120 000

It is estimated the population will increase by 7% in the next year.

Find an estimate for the population of the town in 2024 ⬚

6   18 out of the 40 teachers at a school walk to work.

What percentage of the teachers at the school walk to work? _____

7   A cleaning company increases it's charges from £20 to £25 an hour.

What percentage increase is this? _____

8   Write 249.6 as a percentage of 480 _____

9 An athlete throws a shotput a distance of 20.25 m

   This is an improvement of 8% on their previous throw.

   Calculate the length of their previous throw. [   ] m

10 Dani buys a ticket for a concert for £36

   The price of the ticket had been reduced by 20%

   How much did the ticket originally cost? £ [   ]

11 a) Circle the values that are equivalent to $\frac{4}{10}$

   40%   0.004   0.4 $\frac{2}{5}$ $\frac{10}{4}$ 4% $\frac{5}{2}$

   b) Which value is greater?

      Tick your answer.

      [40% of 40]   [40 reduced by 40%]   [4 increased by 400%]

   c) 4% of 40% of a number is 2

      What is the number? [   ]

12 A car factory produced 480 cars on Thursday.

   The factory was working at 80% capacity that day. This means only 80% of the maximum possible number of cars were produced that day.

   Work out how many cars are made when the factory is working at 95% capacity.

   [   ] cars

How did you find these questions?

Very easy   1   2   3   4   5   6   7   8   9   10   Very difficult

Using percentages

Date:

Let's remember

1   Increase £50 by 10%   £ [ ]

2   Write 160 000 in standard form. _____

3   On the grid, draw a shape congruent to shape A.

4   Solve $2x + 5 = 21$

$x =$ [ ]

Let's practise

1   Without using a calculator, work out 35% of 80 [ ]

2   15% of a number is 90

Work out 70% of the number. [ ]

3   After an increase in sales of 10%, a shop makes £35 200

Mo calculates that before the increase in sales, the shop made
£35 200 − £3520 = £31 680

a) Explain why Mo is wrong.

_____

_____

b) Find the correct amount the shop made before the increase in sales.

_____

_____

4   At a farm, 460 of the 2000 animals are sheep.

What percentage of the animals are sheep?

_____

5   a) How much does this T-shirt cost in the sale?

£ [   ]

b) A jumper costs £62.40 in the same sale.

How much did the jumper cost before the sale?

£ [   ]

6   A company invests some money at 4.5% interest.

After 1 year, their investment is worth £992.75

How much money did the company invest?

£ [   ]

7   When a number is reduced by 15%, the result is 7004

What is the original number?

[   ]

8   Express 258.5 as a percentage of 940 _____

9   Work out 30% of 40% of 50 ⬚

10 A number is increased by 3% and the result is then increased by 3%

H   Which multiplier would you use to find the value after both increases?

Circle your answer.

× 1.3²   × 1.6   × 1.06   × 1.03²

11 There are 2000 bacteria in a test tube.

H   The number of bacteria increases by 20% every hour.

How many bacteria will there be after 3 hours? ⬚

12 a) A number is increased by 40% and the result is decreased by 40%.

H   What percentage of the original number is the final result? _____

b) A number is increased by 25%.

By what percentage must the result be decreased to get back to the original number?

_____

How did you find these questions?

Very easy   1   2   3   4   5   6   7   8   9   10   Very difficult

In this block, you apply some of your number skills to solve problems involving **money**. This is a very useful life skill. You look at **bank statements**, like this one.

Date	Description	Credit (£)	Debit (£)	Balance (£)
22 Jun	Opening balance			165.25
23 Jun	Phone bill		42.56	122.69
24 Jun	Wages	2140.85		2263.54
26 Jun	Card payment		189.99	2073.55

You also look at **simple** and **compound interest**. Which one of these **investments** will earn the most interest?

Bank A - £5000 at 4% simple interest for 6 years

Bank B - £4500 at 3.8% compound interest for 5 years

Another money topic you explore is tax. You learn what the numbers in this table mean.

Band	Taxable income	Tax rates
Personal allowance	Up to €8000	0%
Basic rate	€8000 to €25 000	19%
Higher rate	Over €25 000	35%

You also solve **best value** problems – this is where you **compare** prices to work out which gives you the best deal. Which one of these would *you* buy?

A	B	c
Box of 25 tiles for £7.50	Box of 40 tiles for £11.20	Box of 100 tiles for £29

Key vocabulary

Balance   Debit   Credit   Expense   Interest   Bank statement

Investment   Principal   Deposit   Multiplier   VAT   Value   Salary   Wage

Maths & money

Date:

Let's remember

1 Calculate 4% of £6000 ☐

2 Increase 90 by 40% ☐

3 A textbook costs £11.99

   Find the total cost of 25 textbooks. ☐

4 Work out seven cubed. ☐

Let's practise

1 The table shows the cost per week of staying in a hotel in the summer.

Month	Cost per adult (£)	Cost for children (£)
June	720	Half adult price + £50
July	750	Half adult price + £80
August	780	Half adult price + £100

How much does it cost for a family of two adults and three children to stay in the hotel for 2 weeks in July?

£ ☐

2 Here are two readings from a gas meter.

April   July

a) How many units of gas were used between April and July?

   ☐ units of gas

b) Each unit of gas costs 32p.

   Work out the cost, in pounds, of the gas used between April and July.

   £ ☐

3 Here is part of a bank statement with some values missing.

Date	Description	Credit (£)	Debit (£)	Balance (£)
22 Jun	Opening balance			165.25
23 Jun	Phone bill		42.56	
24 Jun	Wages	2140.85		
26 Jun	Card payment			2073.55

Complete the bank statement.

4 Filip buys a torch and a battery.

The battery costs 5 times as much as the torch.

Filip pays with a £20 note and gets £4.64 change.

How much does the torch cost? £ ▢

5 A bank account pays 6% simple interest per annum.

a) How much interest is paid on £800 after 1 year? £ ▢

b) How much interest is paid on £650 after 3 years? £ ▢

6 A business invests £3000 in a simple interest account.

After 2 years, the investment is worth £3120

What rate of interest did the business receive? _____

7 A company invests £3000 in a bank account that pays 2.5% compound interest per annum.

a) How much money is in the account after

  i) 1 year ▢   ii) 2 years ▢

b) How much interest is paid after 5 years? ▢

8   Find the difference between the interest earned on these investments:

Investment A: £5000 at 4% simple interest for 6 years

Investment B: £4500 at 3.8% compound interest for 5 years

£ [   ]

9   a) A laptop costs £650 plus 20% VAT. Find the total cost of the laptop.

£ [   ]

b) A different laptop costs £840 including 20% VAT. Find the cost of the laptop before VAT is added.

£ [   ]

10   Kim is buying a new car.

The total cost of the car is £9000 plus VAT at 20%

Kim pays a deposit of 15% of the total cost and pays the rest in 12 monthly instalments.

Work out how much Kim pays each month.

£ [   ]

11   An investment of £8000 earns £569.80 after 2 years compound interest.

Work out the interest rate.

_____

How did you find these questions?

Very easy   1   2   3   4   5   6   7   8   9   10   Very difficult

Maths & money

Let's remember

1   Use the exchange rate £1 = $1.32 to change £400 into dollars ($).

$ [   ]

2   50% of a number is 30. What is the number? [   ]

3   Work out $\frac{3}{5} \times \frac{7}{9}$ [   ]

4   Solve $\frac{y}{7} = 10$

$y =$ [   ]

Let's practise

1   The table shows the hourly rates to attend an outdoor pool for different times of the year.

Season	Hourly rate
Autumn	£7.49
Spring	£10.18
Summer	£10.42

a) How much does it cost to use the pool for a total of 36 hours in autumn?

£ [   ]

b) How much does it cost to use the pool for a total of 32 hours in summer?

£ [   ]

2   A rental car costs £555 a week.

A week is calculated as 37 hours.

Calculate the hourly rate. £ [   ]

3 The lease on a shop is £16 200 per year.

How much does it cost per month? £ ▢

4 Last year, a pet shop's total turnover before tax was €40 000

The table shows the tax rates for last year.

Band	Turnover	Tax rates
Small business rate	Up to €50 000	19%
Main rate	Over £250 000	25%

Calculate the pet shop's total tax bill for last year. £ ▢

5 Annie went on holiday to Brunei.

a) She changed £825 into Brunei dollars (BND) when the exchange rate was £1 = 1.72 BND

How many Brunei dollars did she receive? ▢ BND

b) When she returned, she had 326 BND left over. She changed this to British pounds (£) when the exchange rate was £1 = 1.63 BND.

How many British pounds did she receive? £ ▢

6 Rosie bought a car in China for 72 240 Chinese yuan.

When she bought the car, the exchange rate was £1 = 8.40 Chinese yuan.

At the same time, Teddy bought a car in England for £7500

How much more did Rosie spend buying her car than Teddy? £ ▢

7 In December 2022, exchange rates between British pounds (£) and US dollars ($) and between British pounds (£) and euros (€) were

   • £1 = 1.16 US dollars   • £1 = 1.09 euros

   How many euros were 6000 US dollars worth in December 2022?

   Give your answer to the nearest euro.

   €[   ]

8 Find the cost of 1 kg of carrots for each of the offers shown.

   | 8 kg carrots |
   | £3.60 |

   | 15 kg carrots |
   | £6.30 |

   £[   ]   £[   ]

9 Burgers are sold in packets of two different sizes.

   How much cheaper per burger is the larger packet?

   | 15 burgers |
   | £9.30 |

   | 25 burgers |
   | £14.75 |

   £[   ]

10 Two shops have special offers for the same type of shampoo.

Shop A	**Shop B**
£1.80 a bottle	£2.10 a bottle
Buy 3, get 4th free	Buy 2, get 1 free

   Compare the cost per bottle when buying 12 bottles from each shop.

   _____

   _____

   _____

   _____

How did you find these questions?

Very easy   1   2   3   4   5   6   7   8   9   10   Very difficult

Spring term
Block 4   Deduction

In this block, you build on your knowledge of **angles** to solve problems, using **chains of reasoning** – this is also called **deduction**. Start by reminding yourselves about angles in **parallel lines**. Here is an example. Just by knowing that the top angle is 123°, you can work out a, b and c

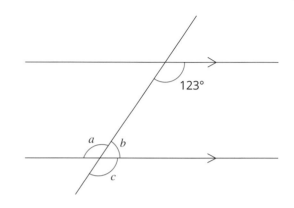

You also look at harder parallel line problems with more than one **transversal**. In this one, you have to solve an equation to work out the unknown angles.

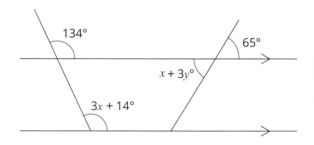

You also explore **conjectures**. That is where there is a statement and you have to say whether it is **true** or **false**. Do you think this conjecture is true or false?

> A quadrilateral cannot have all acute or all obtuse angles.

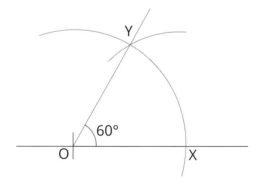

Remember the **constructions** that you learned about last term. In this example, you can use **compasses** to construct an angle of 60°.

Key vocabulary

Angle   Reasoning   Deduction   Parallel lines   Transversal

Conjecture   True   False   Construction   Compasses

Deduction

Date:

Let's remember

1   12 kg of potatoes cost £4.20

How much does 1 kg of potatoes cost?   £ ⬚

2   Increase £800 by 5%   £ ⬚

3   20% of a number is 50

What is the number?   ⬚

4   Write an expression for p multiplied by 7 _____

Let's practise

1   Complete the sentences with either **are equal** or **add up to 180°**

a) Alternate angles in parallel lines _____

b) Corresponding angles in parallel lines _____

c) Co-interior angles in parallel lines _____

d) Vertically opposite angles _____

2   Work out the sizes of angles a, b and c

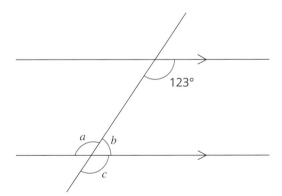

123°

Diagram not drawn accurately

$a =$ _____

$b =$ _____

$c =$ _____

3 Work out the sizes of angles *a*, *b*, *c* and *d*

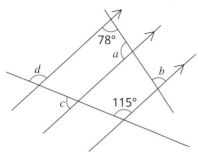

Diagram not drawn accurately

a = _____   *c* = _____

b = _____   *d* = _____

4 Work out the sizes of angles *a*, *b* and *c*

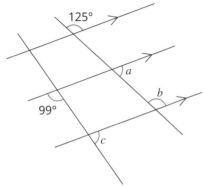

Diagram not drawn accurately

a = _____

b = _____

c = _____

5 Work out the size of angle *a*

Give a reason for each stage of your working.   _____

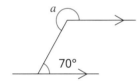
_____

_____

Diagram not drawn accurately   _____

6 Work out the size of angle BAX.

Give a reason for each stage of your working.

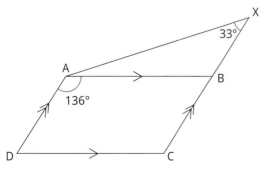

_____

_____

_____

_____

Diagram not drawn accurately

7   AB and CD are parallel. Find the size of angle x

Give a reason for each stage of your working.

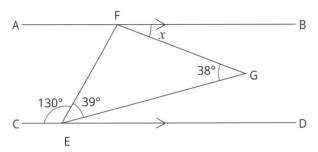

Diagram not drawn accurately

_____

_____

_____

_____

8   AD and EF are parallel. Triangle BEC is isosceles. Find the size of angle y

Give a reason for each stage of your working.

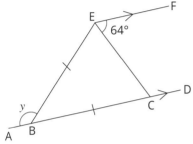

Diagram not drawn accurately

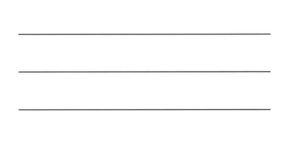

_____

_____

_____

_____

9   Work out the value of x

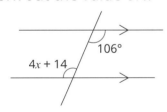

Diagram not drawn accurately

$x =$ ⬚ °

10   The angles in a triangle are $4a - 4$, $4a + 1$, and $5a - 12$

Work out the largest angle in the triangle.

largest angle = ⬚ °

How did you find these questions?

Very easy   1   2   3   4   5   6   7   8   9   10   Very difficult

Deduction

Date:

Let's remember

1   What is the size of angle b?

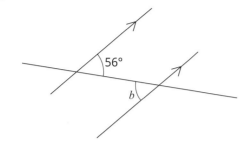

2   Work out 18% of £30 000   £ [   ]

3   Decrease 720 by 10% [   ]

4   Find the volume of the triangular prism. [   ] cm³

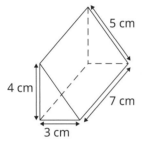

Diagram not drawn accurately

Let's practise

1   Mo conjectures: "Half an obtuse angle is always an acute angle."

   Give **two** examples that support Mo's conjecture.

   _____

   _____

2   Amir conjectures: "Double an acute angle is always an obtuse angle."

   Use a counterexample to show that Amir's conjecture is false.

   _____

   _____

3   Eva conjectures: "If you add a reflex angle to an obtuse angle, the result is greater than a full turn."

a) Give an example that supports Eva's conjecture.

_____

_____

b) Give an example that disproves Eva's conjecture.

_____

_____

4   Here is a conjecture.

> A quadrilateral cannot have all acute or all obtuse angles.

Is the conjecture true or false? Explain your answer.

_____

_____

5   Test this conjecture.

> If you double the lengths of the side of a cube, you double its volume.

_____

_____

6   Show that triangle PQR is isosceles.

Give a reason for each stage of your working.

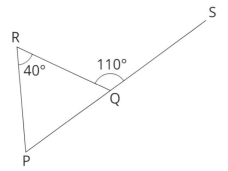

_____

_____

_____

_____

Diagram not drawn accurately

7   Here is a conjecture.

> If you join two congruent triangles by a matching edge, you always get a quadrilateral.

Is the conjecture true or false? _____

Explain your answer.

_____

_____

_____

8   Explain why it is impossible to construct a triangle with sides 12 cm, 8 cm and 3 cm.

_____

_____

9   Explain why it is impossible to construct a triangle with two obtuse angles.

_____

_____

10   Here is a method to construct an angle of 60°

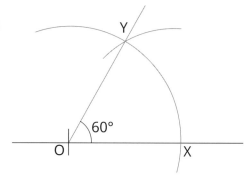

Diagram not drawn accurately

Explain why the method works.

_____

_____

_____

How did you find these questions?

Very easy   1   2   3   4   5   6   7   8   9   10   Very difficult

In this block, you build on what you learned last year about **reflection**, and extend it to **rotation** and **translation**, which are also types of **transformation**. Firstly, you look at **rotational symmetry**, which you can see everywhere, even on road signs.

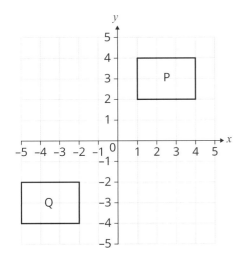

You move on from rotational symmetry to look at **rotation**. You also review and use **coordinate axes**. Rectangle P is called the **object**, and rectangle Q is called the **image** after a rotation.

You also learn about translation. That is when a shape moves vertically and horizontally. The translation from B to A is described by the **vector** $\begin{pmatrix} -3 \\ -2 \end{pmatrix}$

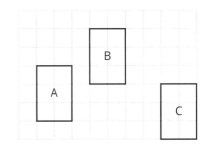

You can combine rotations with the reflections you learned last year. Here, the triangle in the top left has been **transformed** three times to give images A, B and C. Can you see which are rotations and which are reflections?

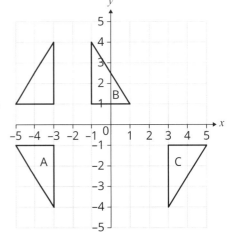

Key vocabulary

Reflection   Rotation   Rotational symmetry   Translation

Vector   Object   Image   Transformation   Coordinate axes

Rotation & translation

Date:

Let's remember

1 An angle measures 205°

   What type of angle is it? _____

2 Two of the angles in a triangle are 70°.

   What is the size of the third angle? ⬜ °

3 Work out 20% of £850

   £ ⬜

4 8 – 20 = ⬜

Let's practise

1 State the order of rotational symmetry for each of the regular shapes.

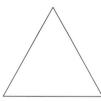   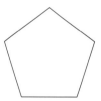   

   _____   _____   _____

2 State the order of rotational symmetry for each letter.

   A   H   K   I   O

   _____   _____   _____   _____   _____

3 Use the grid to draw two shapes with rotational symmetry order 3

4   Shade four squares so that the whole grid has rotational symmetry order 2

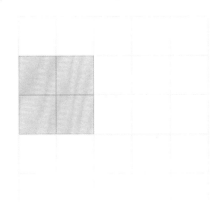

5   Here are some road signs.

A   B   C   D

a) State the order of rotational symmetry for each road sign.

A = _____   B = _____   C = _____   D = _____

b) How many lines of symmetry does each road sign have?

A = _____   B = _____   C = _____   D = _____

6   a) Draw a quadrilateral with 1 line of symmetry and order of rotational symmetry 1

b) Draw a quadrilateral with no lines of symmetry and order of rotational symmetry 1

7   Draw the shapes after a rotation of 90° clockwise.

8   Rotate each shape by 180° about the cross.

a)

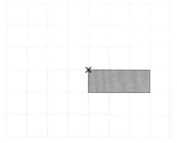

b)

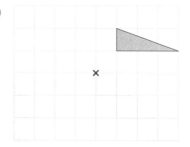

9   Draw each rotation of the rectangle on the coordinate grid.

a) 90° anticlockwise about (0, 1)

b) 180° about (1, 0)

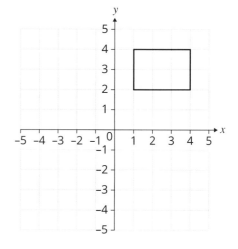

10   Describe fully the single transformation that maps triangle A onto triangle B.

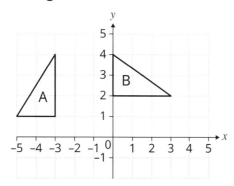

_____

_____

_____

_____

How did you find these questions?

Very easy   1   2   3   4   5   6   7   8   9   10   Very difficult

Rotation & translation

Date:

Let's remember

1 What is the order of rotational symmetry of a square?

2 What is true about corresponding angles?

_____

3 Use the fact that £1 = 42 Thai Baht to change 14 700 Thai Baht to pounds (£).

£

4 Expand and simplify $(y + 5)(y + 10)$

_____

_____

Let's practise

1 Match each column vector to its description.

$\begin{pmatrix} 2 \\ 1 \end{pmatrix}$ 1 right, 2 down

$\begin{pmatrix} 1 \\ -2 \end{pmatrix}$ 2 right, 1 down

$\begin{pmatrix} 2 \\ -1 \end{pmatrix}$ 2 right, 1 up

$\begin{pmatrix} -2 \\ 1 \end{pmatrix}$ 2 left, 1 up

2 Describe the vectors in words.

a) $\begin{pmatrix} -3 \\ 2 \end{pmatrix}$ _____

b) $\begin{pmatrix} 0 \\ -5 \end{pmatrix}$ _____

c) $\begin{pmatrix} 4 \\ 0 \end{pmatrix}$ _____

3 Translate the points by the given vectors.

a) $\begin{pmatrix} -1 \\ 2 \end{pmatrix}$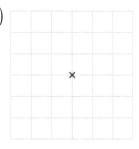

b) $\begin{pmatrix} 2 \\ -1 \end{pmatrix}$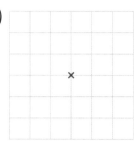

4 Translate the shapes by the given vectors.

a) $\begin{pmatrix} 2 \\ 3 \end{pmatrix}$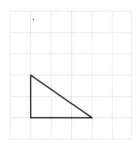

b) $\begin{pmatrix} -2 \\ 1 \end{pmatrix}$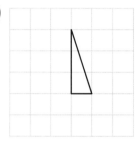

5 Use vector notation to describe the translations.

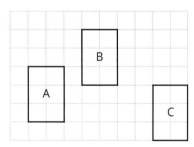

a) A to B _____   c) B to C _____

b) A to C _____   d) C to A _____

6 For each pair of diagrams, decide if B is a reflection of A, a rotation of A or could be either.

a)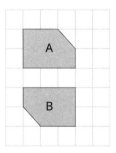

b)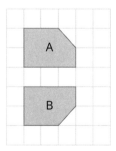

c)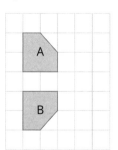

_____   _____   _____

7 A triangle is shown on the grid.

a) Reflect the triangle in the *x*-axis and label the result A.

b) Reflect the triangle in the line *y* = −2 and label the result B.

c) Rotate the triangle 180° about the origin and label the result C.

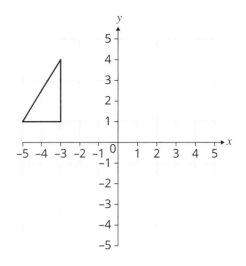

8 Part of a shape is shown on a grid.

The dotted line is a line of symmetry.

a) Complete the shape.

b) Rotate the whole shape by 180° about the origin.

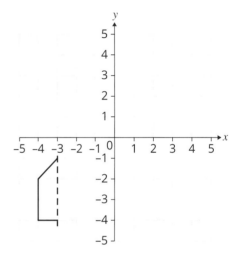

9 Reflect the shape in the *x*-axis and then rotate the result by 180° about the point (1, −1)

H

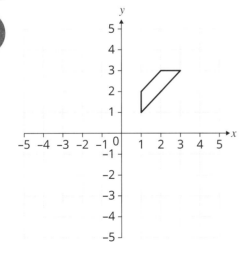

How did you find these questions?

Very easy   1   2   3   4   5   6   7   8   9   10   Very difficult

79

Block 6 Pythagoras' theorem

In this block, you learn about **Pythagoras' theorem**, which is about **right-angled triangles** like this one. You learn about the **hypotenuse**, which is the longest side in a right-angled triangle. In this triangle, which side is the hypotenuse?

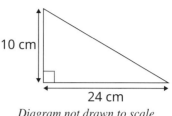

Diagram not drawn to scale

Firstly, here is a reminder about **squares** and **square roots**, which you learned in a previous year. One of these numbers has a positive square root of 14. Do you know which one it is?

| 28 | 7 | 196 | 144 | 3.742 |

You learn to work out the length of a hypotenuse. You have to add together the squares of the two shorter sides and then square root the result. You can use a calculator to work out the length of the hypotenuse of this triangle.

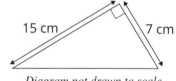

Diagram not drawn to scale

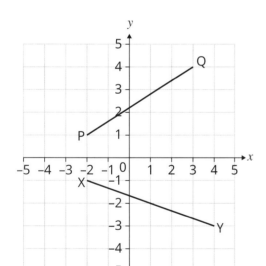

You use Pythagoras' theorem to calculate the length of a **line segment**. Which one of these lines is longer?

Key vocabulary

Pythagoras' theorem   Right-angled triangle   Square   Square root

Hypotenuse   Line segment   Diagonal   Decimal place

Pythagoras' theorem

Date:

Let's remember

1   Describe the vector $\begin{pmatrix} 2 \\ 3 \end{pmatrix}$ in words.

_____

2   How many lines of symmetry does an isosceles trapezium have? ☐

3   Are the labelled angles alternate, corresponding or co-interior? _____

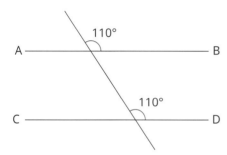

4   −7 × −5 = ☐

Let's practise

1   Work out the square of each number.

a) 8 _____   c) 1.5 _____

b) 12 _____   d) 18 _____

2   Work out the square root of each number.

a) 81 _____   c) 400 _____

b) 121 _____   d) 6.25 _____

3   Write <, > or = to complete the statements.

a) $4^2 + 5^2$ ◯ 9^2 c) 6^2 ◯ $3^2 + 3^2$

b) $3^2 + 4^2$ ◯ 5^2 d) $1^2 + 1^2$ ◯ 2^2

4   Label the hypotenuse of each of these right-angled triangles.

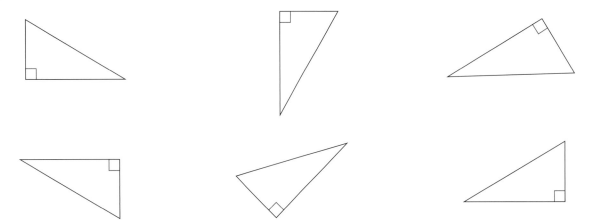

5   The sides of a triangle are 12 cm, 35 cm and 37 cm.

Show that the triangle is right-angled.

_____

_____

_____

6   Use Pythagoras' theorem to determine if these triangles are right-angled.

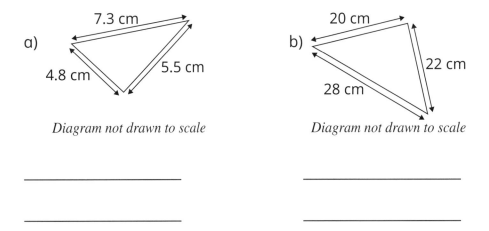

a)

7.3 cm

4.8 cm   5.5 cm

Diagram not drawn to scale

b)

20 cm

28 cm   22 cm

Diagram not drawn to scale

_____   _____

_____   _____

7   Work out the length of the hypotenuse of the right-angled triangle.

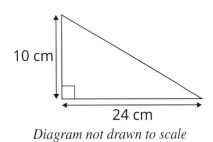

10 cm

24 cm

Diagram not drawn to scale

hypotenuse = [   ] cm

8 Work out the length of the hypotenuse of the right-angled triangle.

Give your answer to 1 decimal place.

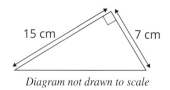

15 cm   7 cm

Diagram not drawn to scale

hypotenuse = [   ] cm

9 A rectangular hockey pitch is 100 yards long and 60 yards wide.

Find the length of the diagonal of the hockey pitch.

Give your answer to 1 decimal place.

diagonal = [   ] yards

10 The sides of a triangle are 5 cm, 12 cm and 14 cm.

Is the triangle right-angled, acute-angled or obtuse-angled?

Explain how you know.

_____

_____

_____

11 The hypotenuse of a right-angled triangle is 40 cm.

The length of the shortest side is 24 cm.

Work out the area of the triangle.

area = [   ] cm^2

How did you find these questions?

Very easy   1   2   3   4   5   6   7   8   9   10   Very difficult

Pythagoras' theorem

Date:

Let's remember

1 Label the hypotenuse on the right-angled triangle.

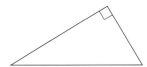

2 Describe the vector $\begin{pmatrix} 4 \\ -1 \end{pmatrix}$ in words.

_____

3 Increase £700 by 20%   £ [ ]

4 Are the triangles congruent? Explain your answer.

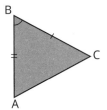 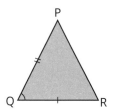

_____

Let's practise

1 Here is a triangle XYZ.

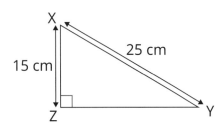

25 cm

15 cm

Diagram not drawn accurately

a) Which side is the hypotenuse? _____

b) Work out the length of the side ZY.

ZY = [ ] cm

2   Dora is working out the length of BC in this triangle.

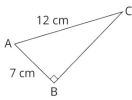

Diagram not drawn accurately

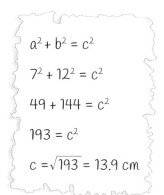

$a^2 + b^2 = c^2$

$7^2 + 12^2 = c^2$

$49 + 144 = c^2$

$193 = c^2$

$c = \sqrt{193} = 13.9$ cm

What mistake has Dora made?

_____

3   Work out the length of the unknown side in each triangle.

a)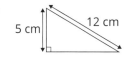

Diagram not drawn to scale

b)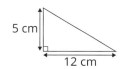

Diagram not drawn to scale

4   The length of the hypotenuse of a right-angled isosceles triangle is 12 cm.

Work out the length of one of the shorter sides of the triangle.

Give your answer to 1 decimal place.

[   ] cm

5   Triangle ABC is drawn on a 1-centimetre coordinate grid.

a) Write the lengths of

i) AB [   ] cm   ii) BC [   ] cm

b) Work out the length of AC correct to 1 decimal place.

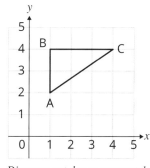

Diagram not drawn accurately

AC = [   ] cm

85

6 Work out the lengths of the line segments PQ and XY.

Give your answers to 1 decimal place.

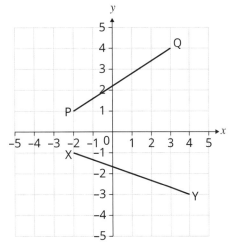

Diagram not drawn accurately

7 The diagram shows a rectangle and a triangle joined to make a trapezium.

AB = 12 cm, BC = 5 cm and EC = 15 cm

Work out the area of the trapezium.

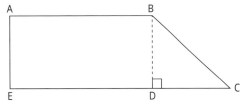

Diagram not drawn accurately

8 ABCDEFGH is a cuboid.

H

Which of the following are right-angled triangles?

Circle your answers.

ABC   ECF   AEG   FHB   HAG

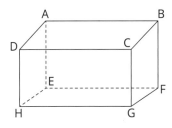

Diagram not drawn accurately

9 Work out the length of the longest diagonal of a cube with sides of 8 cm.

H

Give your answer correct to 1 decimal place.

How did you find these questions?

Very easy   1   2   3   4   5   6   7   8   9   10   Very difficult

Spring term   Self-assessment

Time to reflect

Look back through the work you have done this term. Think about what you enjoyed and what you found easy or hard. Talk about this to your teacher and someone at home.

Try these questions	How do you feel about this topic? Tick the box.
A jacket is in a sale. What was the price of the jacket before the sale? £ [＿＿＿＿＿] **Sale 25% off!** Now only £45 If you need a reminder, look back at percentages on pages 53–58	☐ I am confident and could teach someone else. ☐ I think I understand but I need practice. ☐ I don't understand and need help.
Rotate the triangle ABC 90° clockwise about the point (–1, 0). If you need a reminder, look back at rotation on pages 74–79	☐ I am confident and could teach someone else. ☐ I think I understand but I need practice. ☐ I don't understand and need help.
Calculate the length of AC. Give your answer in centimetres to 1 decimal place. 6 cm, 12 cm AC = [＿＿＿＿＿] cm If you need a reminder, look back at Pythagoras' theorem on pages 81–86	☐ I am confident and could teach someone else. ☐ I think I understand but I need practice. ☐ I don't understand and need help.

Block 1 Enlargement & similarity

In this block, you extend what you know about **transformations** to **enlargement**. This is all about using **scaling** to change the size of a shape. You start by learning a new word, **similarity**. In this diagram, three of the rectangles are similar to rectangle X. Can you work out which ones they are?

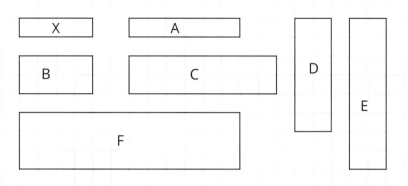

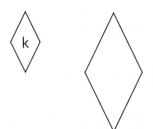

You enlarge shapes by a **scale factor**. Rhombus K has been enlarged by **scale factor 2**.

You also enlarge shapes on **coordinate axes**. Here is an example of a triangle that you can enlarge by scale factor $\frac{1}{2}$, which actually means its image will be smaller.

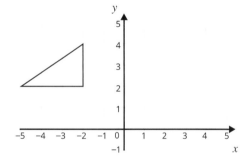

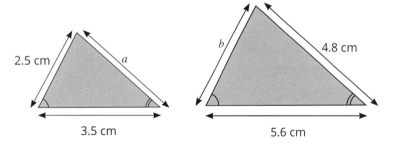

2.5 cm a

3.5 cm

b 4.8 cm

5.6 cm

Diagram not drawn accurately

You explore **similar triangles**, and use them to work out the size of missing angles or lengths. Here is an example.

Key vocabulary

Similar   Enlargement   Ratio   Scale factor   Object

Image   Centre   Corresponding

Enlargement & similarity

Date:

Let's remember

1   The shorter sides of a right-angled triangle measure 30 cm and 40 cm.

What is the length of the hypotenuse? ☐ cm

2   Write the vector to show a translation that is 5 to the right and 3 down. _____

3   How many lines of symmetry does a regular hexagon have? ☐

4   Work out $(-7)^2$ ☐

Let's practise

1   Tick the shapes that are similar to rectangle X.

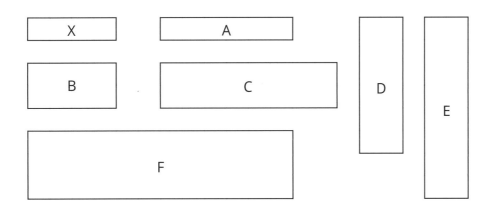

2   Draw two rectangles that are similar to rectangle A.

A

3 Are the parallelograms similar? _____

Explain your answer.

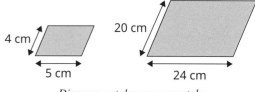

4 cm

20 cm

5 cm

24 cm

Diagram not drawn accurately

_____

_____

_____

4 Enlarge the shape by scale factor 3

5 Enlarge the shape by scale factor 2

6 A rectangle has a length of 8 cm and a width of 5 cm.

It is enlarged by scale factor 6

What are the dimensions of the enlarged rectangle?

_____

_____

7 Enlarge the triangle by scale factor 2, using the cross as the centre of enlargement.

8   Enlarge the shape by scale factor 3, using the cross as the centre of enlargement.

9   Enlarge the triangle by scale factor $\frac{1}{2}$, using (0, 0) as the centre of enlargement.

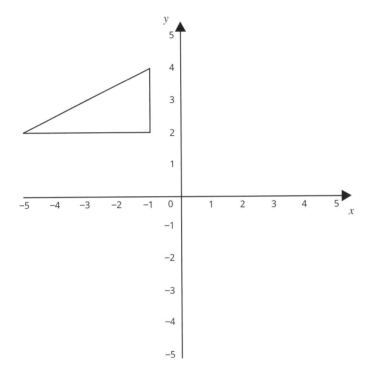

10 Rectangle A has a length of 18 cm and a width of 12 cm.

Rectangle B has a length of 12 cm and a width of 8 cm.

Is rectangle B an enlargement of rectangle A? Justify your answer.

_____

_____

_____

How did you find these questions?

Very easy   1   2   3   4   5   6   7   8   9   10   Very difficult

Enlargement & similarity

Date:

Let's remember

1   A rectangle is 7 cm long and 5 cm wide. The rectangle is enlarged by a scale factor of 10. What are the dimensions of the enlarged rectangle?

length = [   ] cm   width = [   ] cm

2   The two longest sides of a right-angled triangle are 20 cm and 25 cm.

Find the length of the shortest side of the triangle.   [   ] cm

3   Describe in words the translation described by the vector $\begin{pmatrix} 0 \\ -3 \end{pmatrix}$

_____

4   Write 6.8×10^4 as an ordinary number   [   ]

Let's practise

1   These two rectangles are similar.

a) What is the scale factor of the
   enlargement from A to B?   [   ]

b) Work out the value of x [   ]

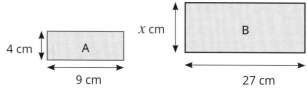

4 cm   A   9 cm

x cm   B   27 cm

Diagram not drawn accurately

2   A and B are similar triangles.

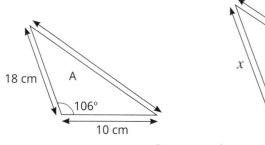

18 cm   A   106°   10 cm

x B y 25 cm

Diagram not drawn accurately

a) What is the scale factor of the enlargement from A to B?   [   ]

b) Work out the length of the side labelled x [   ] cm

c) Work out the value of y [   ] °

3   Here are two similar triangles.

Work out the value of a

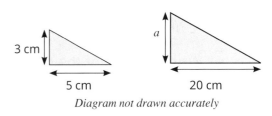

Diagram not drawn accurately

[   ] cm

4   Here are two similar rectangles.

Work out the length of the side labelled x

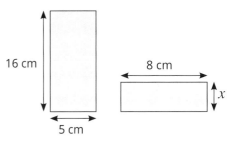

Diagram not drawn accurately

[   ] cm

5   Enlarge the shape by scale factor −2, using the cross as the centre of enlargement.

H

6   Enlarge the triangle by scale factor −1,
using the origin as the centre of enlargement.

H

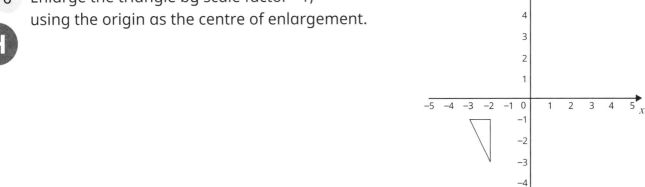

7   Here are two similar triangles.

H

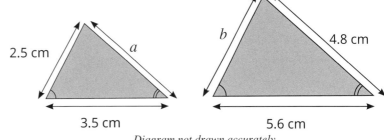

Diagram not drawn accurately

Work out the lengths of the sides labelled a and b

$a =$ [   ] cm $b =$ [   ] cm

93

8   Here are two similar triangles.

H

a) Write the size of the angle labelled x

$x = $ ⬚ °

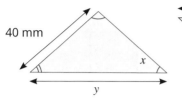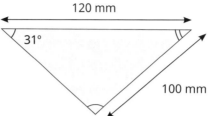

Diagram not drawn accurately

b) Work out the length of the side labelled y

$y = $ ⬚ mm

9   These right-angled triangles are similar.

H

a) Work out the value of a

$a = $ ⬚

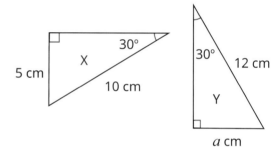

Diagram not drawn accurately

b) Which of the triangles below are also similar to X and Y?

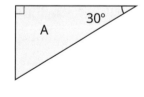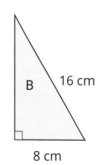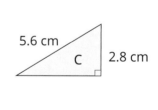

How did you find these questions?

Very easy   1   2   3   4   5   6   7   8   9   10   Very difficult

Block 2 Solving ratio & proportion problems

In this block, you extend your knowledge of **direct proportion**, so that you can solve lots of real-life problems. For example, in this recipe can you make 32 pancakes with 200 g of butter?

Ingredients to make
4 pancakes

55 g plain flour
1 egg
100 ml milk
37.5 ml water
25 g butter

You can represent **linear relationships**, using **graphs**. You can work out which of these graphs show direct proportion.

A

B

C

D

You use a **table of values** to show **inverse proportion**, like this for example. As A goes up, B goes down – and as B goes up, A goes down.

A	1	2	4	8	25
B	40	20	10	5	1.6

You revisit the work you did on 'best buy' problems last term, and look at a new way to solve them, using **scaling**. Which of these offers do you think is better **value** for money?

£1.80
Buy 1 get 1 free

£1.50
Buy 2 get 1 free

Key vocabulary

Direct proportion   Linear relationship   Graph   Table of values

Inverse proportion   Scaling   Value   Ratio

Solving ratio & proportion problems

Date:

Let's remember

1   The angles in a triangle are 50°, 60° and 70°

What are the sizes of the angles if the triangle is enlarged by scale factor 3?

_____

2   A square with side length 3 cm is enlarged by scale factor 4

What is the side length of the enlarged square? [   ] cm

3   Work out $\sqrt{20^2 - 12^2}$ [   ]

4   Write 4.5% as a decimal. [   ]

Let's practise

1   A 3 m length of wire costs 85p

Work out the cost of

a) a 6 m length of the same wire   £ [   ]

b) a 60 m length of the same wire   £ [   ]

2   In a zoo, the animals eat 312 kg of food over 4 days.

How much food would the animals eat in

a) 12 days? [   ] kg

b) 2 days? [   ] kg

c) 10 days? [   ] kg

3   5 school chairs have a total mass of 16 kg.

a) What is the mass of 25 school chairs? [   ] kg

b) The mass of a stack of chairs is 48 kg. How many chairs are in the stack?

[   ]

c) Work out the mass of one chair. [   ] kg

4   Here is a recipe for pancakes.

Ingredients to make
4 pancakes

60 g plain flour
1 egg
100 ml milk
40 ml water
35 g butter

a) How much butter is needed for 12 pancakes?

g

b) How many pancakes can you make with 360 g of flour?

5   16 miles is approximately 14 nautical miles.

a) Use this information to draw a conversion graph.

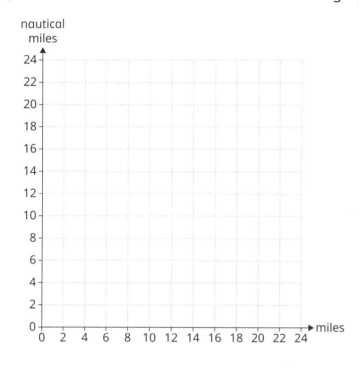

b) Use your graph to complete the approximate conversions.

10 miles ≈ nautical miles

20 nautical miles ≈ miles

c) Convert 200 miles to nautical miles.

200 miles ≈ nautical miles

6   Tick the graphs that show direct proportion relationships.

A

B

C

D

7   Three trucks of equal size take 12 hours to move 250 tons of materials. How long
would it take nine trucks of the same size to do the same job?

8   It takes 4 hours to empty a tank, using 20 identical pumps.

a) How long would it take using 5 of these pumps? ☐ hours

b) How many pumps would you need to empty the tank in 1 hour? ☐

9   A is inversely proportional to B.

Complete the table.

A	1	2	4	8	25
B		20		5	

10   Tick the graphs that show inverse proportion relationships.

A

B

C

D

11   The time taken by cows to eat all the grass in a field is inversely proportional to the
number of cows in the field.

When there are 15 cows in the field, the time taken to eat the grass is 48 days.

Find the greatest number of cows that should be allowed in the field if the grass is to

last 40 days. ☐

How did you find these questions?

Very easy   1   2   3   4   5   6   7   8   9   10   Very difficult

Solving ratio & proportion problems

Date:

Let's remember

1 7 booklets cost £20. How much will 21 booklets cost? £ ☐

2 A square with side length 5 cm is enlarged by scale factor 3
   What is the perimeter of the enlarged square? ☐ cm

3 The hypotenuse of a right-angled triangle is 25 cm.
   The length of the shortest side is 15 cm.
   What is the length of the other side? ☐ cm

4 25% of ☐ = 45

Let's practise

1 Esther and Filip share £80 in the ratio 2:3
   How much do they each receive?
   Esther £ ☐   Filip £ ☐

2 Some pastry is made of flour and butter. The ratio of flour to butter in the pastry is 2:1
   a) How much butter is needed to make 150 g of pastry? ☐ g

   b) How much butter is needed with 150 g of flour? ☐ g

   c) How much pastry is made if there is 150 g more flour than butter? ☐ g

3   The angles in a triangle are in the ratio 3:4:5

Show that all the angles in the triangle are acute.

4   Paint costs £12 for a 5-litre tin and £8 for a 3-litre tin.

Which tin is better value for money? Show all your working.

The _____ is better value for money.

5   Which is better value for money?

Tick your answer.

Show all your working.

| Potatoes 450 g for 25p | Potatoes 1 kg for 58p |

6   Mo needs to buy 6 litres of apple juice.

Which deal is better value for money?

Tick your answer.

Show all your working.

7 Dexter needs to buy 120 party poppers.

The Party Company Party poppers 15p each Buy 8, get 2 extra free	Super Party Party poppers £2.95 for a pack of 24

Which company offers the cheapest price and by how much?

Show all your working.

_____ is cheapest and by £ [   ]

8 $a:b = 3:2$

H

$a + b = 60$

Work out the values of a and b

$a =$ [   ] $b =$ [   ]

9 The ratio of $x:y$ is $4:5$

H

Tick the statements that are always true.

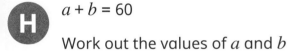

$y > x$ $\dfrac{x}{y} = \dfrac{4}{5}$ $x = \dfrac{5}{4}y$ $x + y = 9$ $5x = 4y$

10 The ratio of the sum of x and y to the difference between x and y is $4:3$

H

Show that x is 7 times the size of y.

How did you find these questions?

Very easy   1   2   3   4   5   6   7   8   9   10   Very difficult

Summer term
Block 3   Rates

In this block, you build on the work you have recently done on **direct** and **inverse proportion**, and apply it to **rates**. You start by learning about the relationship between **speed**, **distance** and **time**. If a motorbike travels at a **constant** speed of 40 miles per hour, you can show it on a double number line.

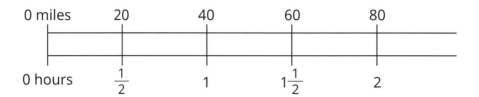

You explore **distance–time graphs**. You use these to tell the story of a journey. Here is part of the journey of a car over the first 80 seconds. Can you see when it travels at its fastest speed?

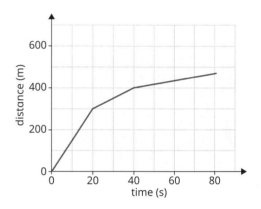

You look at other kinds of rates, like water flowing into a tank for example. Here are four different graphs representing water flowing at different rates. The one on the left starts with a fast **flow rate** and then slows right down.

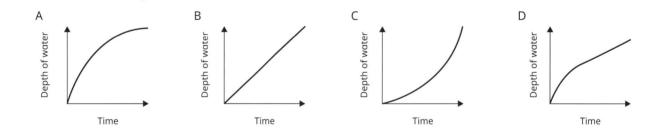

You also look at **density**, which measures the relationship between the mass and volume of a substance. Did you know that an object will float on water if its density is lower than that of water, which is 1 g/cm³?

Key vocabulary

Direct proportion   Inverse proportion   Rate   Speed   Distance   Time

Constant   Distance–time graph   Gradient   Flow rate   Density

Rates

Date:

Let's remember

1 Share £40 in the ratio 5 : 3

£ [ ] : £ [ ]

2 10 pens cost £3.50

How much do 15 pens cost?   £ [ ]

3 A shape has height 18 cm.

The shape is enlarged by scale factor 5

What is the height of the enlarged shape?   [ ] cm

4 Find the cost of 856 units of gas at 18.5p per unit.   £ [ ]

Let's practise

1 A drone flies 120 m in 15 seconds.

Find the average speed of the drone in metres per second.   [ ] m/s

2 A bus leaves at 14:45 and arrives at its destination, 180 km away, at 17:15

Work out the average speed of the bus in km/h.   [ ] km/h

3 Kim drove for 3 hours at an average speed of 40 mph to get to a meeting.

Her journey home on the same route took 5 hours.

Calculate Kim's average speed, in miles per hour, on the way home.   [ ] mph

4   A motorbike travels 30 miles in 25 minutes.

Work out the average speed of the motorbike in miles per hour.   ☐ mph

5   A lorry drives 322 miles from Gateshead to Gatwick.

The journey takes 7 hours and 45 minutes.

a) Write 7 hours and 45 minutes as a decimal.   ☐ hours

b) Calculate the average speed of the lorry, in miles per hour.

Give your answer to 1 decimal place.   ☐

6   Ron's journey to work is 6.6 miles.

His average speed for the journey is 22 mph.

a) How long, in hours, does the journey take?   ☐ hours

b) Convert your answer to part a) to minutes.   ☐ minutes

7   Here is part of a distance–time graph of a car's journey.

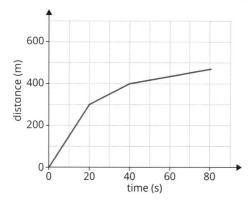

a) Between which two times was the car travelling at its greatest speed?
    Give a reason for your answer.

_____

_____

b) Calculate the car's greatest speed.   ☐ m/s

8   The distance–time graph shows part of a bike ride.

   a) Describe what is happening between
       9:45 am and 10 am

   _____

   b) Calculate the speed of the bike in the first
       45 minutes of the ride.

   [_____] km/h

9   A cuboid measures 10 cm by 8 cm by 6 cm and
    has mass 816 g.

   a) Work out the volume of the cuboid.

   [_____] cm³

   b) Calculate the density of the cuboid, stating units with your answer.

   _____

10   A block of metal has density 3.7 g/cm³ The volume of the block is 18 000 cm³

   Calculate the mass of the block in kilograms.

   [_____] kg

11   100 g of lead is mixed with 200 g of tin to make an alloy.

   Lead has a density of 11.3 g/cm³ and tin has a density of 7.3 g/cm³

   Work out the mass of 30 cm³ of the alloy.

   [_____] g

How did you find these questions?

Very easy   1   2   3   4   5   6   7   8   9   10   Very difficult

Rates

Date:

Let's remember

1   A car travels 50 miles in 2 hours.

What is the average speed of the car?   [   ] mph

2   8 light bulbs cost £6

How much do 10 light bulbs cost?   £ [   ]

3   Are the rectangles similar?

_____

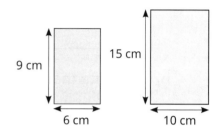

9 cm

15 cm

6 cm

10 cm

4   Use the exchange rate £1 = €1.13 to change €2599 to pounds (£).

£ [   ]

Let's practise

1   300 litres of petrol is pumped into a tank in 4 minutes.

Find the rate of the flow of petrol.

a)   [   ] litres per minute

b)   [   ] litres per second

2   Water flows into a pond at a rate of 50 litres per minute.

a) How much water flows into the pond in 1 hour?   [   ] litres

b) How much water flows into the pond in 15 seconds?   [   ] litres

3   a) Which of the graphs show water flowing into a cuboid tank at a constant rate?

Tick your answer.

A
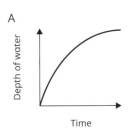

B
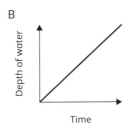

C
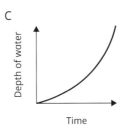

D
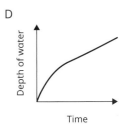

b) Describe how the rate of flow changes for the other three graphs.

_____

_____

_____

4   A machine fills 3000 bottles of water in 1 hour.

a) How many bottles are filled in 1 minute?

b) How many minutes does the machine take to fill 400 bottles?

minutes

5   Aisha can type 700 words in 20 minutes.

Jack can type 950 words in 25 minutes.

Who types faster, and by how much? _____

6   A machine fills trays of 30 pots with yoghurt.

In 2 hours, the machine fills a total of 36 000 pots.

How long does the machine take to fill each tray of 30 pots?

Give your answer in seconds.   s

7   5 miles ≈ 8 kilometres

   a) Convert 40 miles to kilometres.   b) Convert 40 kilometres to miles.

   ☐ km   ☐ miles

   c) Annie is driving along a road in France, which has a speed limit of 80 km per hour.

   She is driving at 45 mph. By how much is her speed above or below the speed limit?

   ☐ mph

8   The density of tin is 7300 kg/m³

(H) What is the density of tin in g/cm³?   ☐ g/cm³

9   A car is travelling along a motorway at 90 km/h.

   The time taken to travel between two bridges is 15 seconds.

   Work out the distance between the two bridges in metres.   ☐ m

10   During June, Nijah drove a distance of 800 miles in her car.

   Her car's fuel consumption was 42 miles per gallon.

   Petrol cost £1.58 per litre.

   1 gallon is approximately 4.55 litres.

   Calculate the cost of the petrol Nijah used in June.   £ ☐

   How did you find these questions?

   Very easy   1   2   3   4   5   6   7   8   9   10   Very difficult

Summer term
Block 4   Probability

In this block, you build on the work you have done in previous years on **probability**. It is important that you know that the probability of an **event** is measured on a scale from 0 to 1, as shown in this **number line**. Here, event B is impossible.

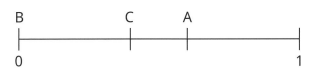

Number of throws	20	40	60
Number of heads	7	18	24
Relative frequency	0.35	0.45	0.4

You **estimate** probability by performing an **experiment** and calculating **relative frequency**. Just like experiments in science, you do something and then record the result. You can use a **table** to represent the results.

You use **tree diagrams** to list **outcomes** from **combined events**, and to help calculate probabilities. This tree diagram shows the results of archery target practice. You can write in the probabilities along the branches.

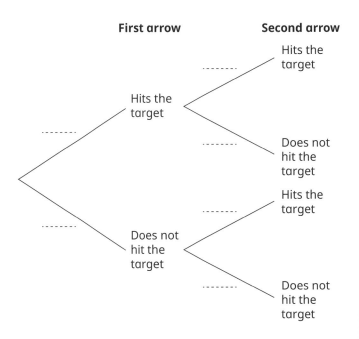

You also use **Venn diagrams** to help you organise information and to help work out probabilities. This one shows that the probability that a **randomly** chosen student studies English is $\frac{26}{50}$. Can you see how to work that out?

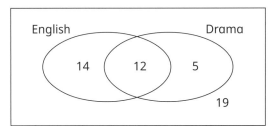

Key vocabulary

Probability

Date:

Let's remember

1. Water flows into a litre tank at a rate of 25 litres per minute.

   How much water will be in the tank after 10 minutes? [＿＿＿＿] litres

2. A car travels 90 miles in 3 hours. Work out the average speed of the car.

   [＿＿＿＿] mph

3. The total mass of 8 identical boxes is 2800 g.

   What is the total mass of 5 of the boxes? [＿＿＿＿] g

4. Share £50 in the ratio 1 : 4

   £ [＿＿＿＿] : £ [＿＿＿＿]

Let's practise

1. Complete the probabilities for the events in the table.

Event	Probability
Getting tails on a single throw of a coin	
Choosing Friday when selecting a day at random from the days of the week	
Choosing M when selecting a letter at random from the word MATHEMATICS	

2. Mo has these eight cards.

   Mo picks one card at random.

   | 5 | 6 | 7 | 8 | 9 | 10 | 11 | 12 |

   On the probability scale below, mark the points A, B and C where

   • A is the probability that Mo chooses an odd number

   • B is the probability that Mo chooses a number less than 4

   • C is the probability that Mo chooses a factor of 24

   0 ———————————————————————————————— 1

3 A bag contains only red and green counters.

The ratio of red counters to green counters in the bag is $3:5$

What is the probability that a counter picked at random from the bag is green?

_____

4 In a school, there are six classes in Year 9. There are 30 students in each class.

The number of students who have pet dogs in each class is 4, 6, 3, 2, 7 and 5

Work out the best estimate of the relative frequency of randomly selecting a student who has a pet dog from one of the classes.

_____

5 A biased coin is thrown 100 times.

The running total of the number of heads thrown is recorded after each 20 throws.

Number of throws	20	40	60	80	100
Number of heads	7	18	24		
Relative frequency	0.35			0.4	0.42

a) Some of the results are shown in the table. Complete the table.

b) Write the best estimate of the probability of throwing a head. _____

6 A ten-sided spinner is labelled with the numbers from 1 to 10

The spinner is spun 20 times and lands on 1 six times.

The spinner is spun a further 20 times and lands on 1 five times.

Do you think the spinner is fair? Explain your answer.

_____

_____

7 A biased die is rolled 150 times. The probability that the die lands on 6 is 0.3

How many times would you expect the die to land on 6?

_____ times

8 A box contains five balls labelled 0, 1, 2, 3 and 4

One ball is chosen at random from the box, its number is recorded and it is then placed back in the box. This is repeated 200 times.

How many times would you expect an odd-numbered ball to be chosen?

┌──────────┐
│   │ times
└──────────┘

9 Filip has these cards in a bag.

M A T H S

Huan has these cards in a bag.

S U M S

Filip and Huan both select a card at random and replace them in their bags 100 times.

How many more times would you expect Huan to select an S than Filip?

┌──────────┐
│   │
└──────────┘

10 A fair coin is flipped and a fair die numbered 1 to 6 is rolled.

Calculate the probability that the coin shows heads and the dice shows a 5

probability = _____

11 The events A and B are independent. P(A) = 0.6 and P(B) = 0.3

What is the probability that neither A nor B occur?

probability = _____

How did you find these questions?

Very easy   1   2   3   4   5   6   7   8   9   10   Very difficult

Probability

Date:

Let's remember

1 What is the probability of a fair dice landing on 5? $\frac{\square}{\square}$

2 A car travels 18 miles in half an hour.

What is the average speed of the car? [   ] mph

3 The ratio of red to green buttons in a jar is 2:3

There are 120 green buttons in the jar. How many red buttons are there?

[   ] buttons

4 Expand and simplify $(t + 9)(t - 1)$

_____

_____

Let's practice

1 Each time Sam fires an arrow at a target, the probability it hits the target is 0.7

H

Sam fires two arrows at the target.

a) Complete the tree diagram.

b) Calculate the probability Sam hits the target both times.

_____

c) Calculate the probability Sam misses the target both times.

_____

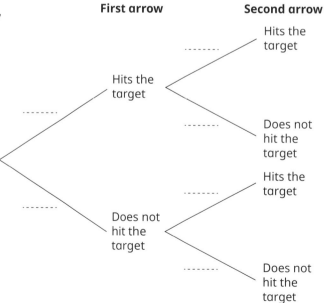

113

2 At a shop, 60% of the skirts are red and the rest are blue.

H

30% of the blue skirts and 45% of the red skirts have a pocket.

a) Complete the tree diagram to show this information.

b) One skirt is selected at random. What is the probability that it has a pocket?

Red

Has a pocket

Does not have a pocket

Blue

Has a pocket

Does not have a pocket

3 Jack is visiting Paris. The probability he will go to the Eiffel Tower is 0.8 and the probability he will go to Notre Dame is 0.4. The two events are independent.

H

Calculate the probability that Jack will go to either the Eiffel Tower or to Notre Dame but not both.

probability = _____

4 A bag contains 7 red and 3 green sweets.

H

Kim selects a sweet at random and eats it.

She then selects another sweet at random and eats it.

a) Complete the tree diagram to show the colours of sweets picked.

b) Calculate the probability that Kim eats two sweets of the same colour.

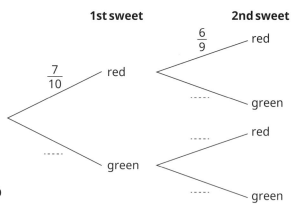

1st sweet   **2nd sweet**

$\frac{7}{10}$ red

$\frac{6}{9}$ red

green

green

red

green

probability = _____

5 A bowl contains 13 blue and 7 yellow marbles.

Two marbles are selected at random, without replacement.

Calculate the probability that the marbles are of different colours.

probability = _____

6 The table shows the number of Year 9 and Year 10 athletes competing at different events in a competition.

	Track event	Field event	Total
Year 9	7	13	20
Year 10	14	11	25
Total	21	24	45

a) What is the probability that an athlete selected at random is in Year 9?

probability = _____

b) What is the probability that a track event athlete selected at random is in Year 10?

probability = _____

7 The Venn diagram shows some information about the subjects studied by 50 students in a sixth-form college.

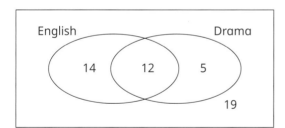

One student is selected at random.

a) What is the probability they study both English and Drama? _____

b) What is the probability they study English but not Drama? _____

c) Given that the student studies Drama, what is the probability they also study English? _____

How did you find these questions?

Very easy   1   2   3   4   5   6   7   8   9   10   Very difficult

115

Block 5 Algebraic representation

In this block, you represent **equations** and **inequalities**, using **graphs**. This builds on the work you did in the autumn, and allows you to explore graphs that are not straight lines, like these.

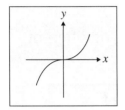 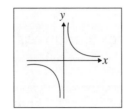 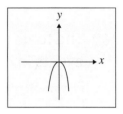

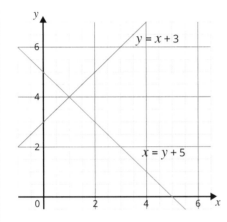

You use graphs to solve **simultaneous equations**, like these. If you have two equations that are represented by graphs, you just look for their **intersection**, and that is the **solution**.

You use **number lines** to represent **inequalities**, like this one. The open circle means that it does not include −1

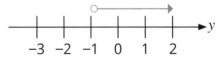

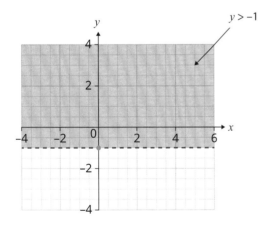

You can also show inequalities, using a graph. This graph is another way of representing the inequality shown on the number line above.

Key vocabulary

Equation   Inequality   Graph   Simultaneous equations

Solution   Intersection   Inequality   Quadratic

Algebraic representation

Date:

Let's remember

1   The table shows the results of some students in two tests.

	English	French	Total
Pass	19	18	37
Fail	11	15	26
Total	30	33	63

What is the probability a randomly selected student failed their test? _____

2   A fair six-sided die is rolled 600 times.

How many times would you expect it to land on 1?

3   Water flows into a tank at a rate of 25 litres per minute.

After how many minutes will there be 500 litres of water in the tank?

4   What is the order of rotational symmetry of a trapezium?

Let's practise

1   The table shows some of the values of $y = x^2 - 2x - 4$ for x-values from −3 to 4

x	−3	−2	−1	0	1	2	3	4
$y = x^2 - 2x - 4$	11	4	−1					4

a) Complete the table.

b) Draw the graph of $y = x^2 - 2x - 4$ on the coordinate axes.

c) Use your graph to estimate the values of x
   when $x^2 - 2x - 4 = 0$

$x =$ _____ $x =$ _____

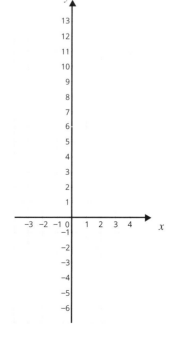

117

2   Match the graphs to the equations.

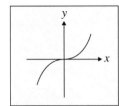   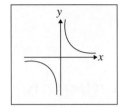   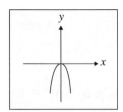

$$y = \frac{1}{x}$$ $$y = -x^2$$ $$y = x^3$$

3   Here are the graphs of $y = x + 3$ and $x + y = 5$

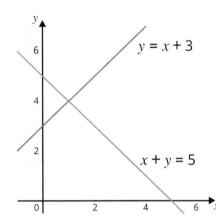

Use the graphs to find the solution to the simultaneous equations
$y = x + 3$ and $x + y = 5$

$x =$ ☐

$y =$ ☐

4   Circle the correct solution to the simultaneous equations $x + y = 7$, $y = 2x + 1$

    $x = 5, y = 2$ $x = 2, y = 5$ $x = 1, y = 6$ $x = 6, y = 1$

5   Write the inequalities shown by the number lines.

a)   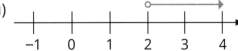   b)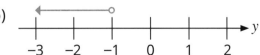

_____   _____

6 Draw the inequalities on the number lines.

a) $x < 1$

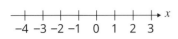

b) $-3 < x \leq 2$

7 Draw the inequalities on the grids.

a) $y \leq 2$

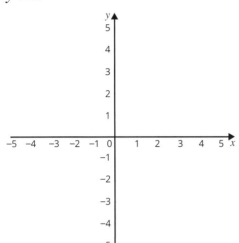

b) $x > 2$

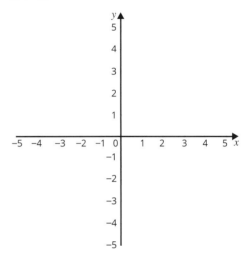

8 Write three inequalities to describe the **unshaded** region.

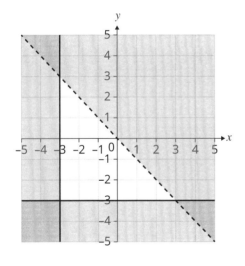

_____

_____

_____

How did you find these questions?

Very easy   1   2   3   4   5   6   7   8   9   10   Very difficult

Revision of sequences & indices

Date:

Let's remember

1   Write three integers that satisfy the inequality $x < 9$

_____

2   The probability that Mo is late for school on any day is 0.1

What is the probability that Mo is not late for school? _____

3   A car travels at a constant speed of 30 mph for 5 hours.

How far does it travel? [ ] miles

4   Describe the translation given by the vector $\begin{pmatrix} 4 \\ -3 \end{pmatrix}$ in words.

_____

Let's practise

1   The nth term of a sequence is given by the rule $3n + 1$

a) Use $n = 1$ to work out the first term of the sequence. [ ]

b) Work out the 5th term of the sequence. [ ]

c) Work out the 100th term of the sequence. [ ]

2   Tick the **linear** sequences.

| **A:** | 1 | 5 | 9 | 13 |

| **B:** | 10 | 8 | 6 | 4 |

| **C:** | 1 | 2 | 4 | 8 |

| **D:** | 1 | 4 | 9 | 16 |

| **E:** | 6.1 | 6.3 | 6.5 | 6.7 |

120

3   Teddy thinks all the terms in the sequence given by the rule $2n + 4$ are even.

Is Teddy correct? Justify your answer.

_____

_____

4   The nth term of a sequence is given by the rule $n(n + 1)$

a) Show that the 3rd term of the sequence is 12

b) Work out the 10th term of the sequence. ☐

c) Is the sequence linear? Explain your answer.

_____

_____

5   Work out the rule for the nth term of each sequence.

a) 10, 15, 20, 25...   b) 1, 5, 9, 13...   c) 98, 96, 94, 92...

_____   _____   _____

6   Here is a way of arranging chairs around rows of 1, 2 and 3 tables.

a) Draw the same arrangement for a row of 4 tables.

b) Find a rule for the number of chairs when there are n tables.

_____

_____

c) How many tables are needed for 62 chairs? ☐

7 Work out

a) $2^3 = $ ___

b) $3^4 = $ ___

c) $1^7 = $ ___

8 Complete the calculations.

a) ___$^3 = 125$

b) $2^{\boxed{}} = 32$

c) $10^{\boxed{}} = 100\,000$

9 Simplify the expressions.

a) $a^5 \times a^7 = $ _____

b) $b^{10} \div b^2 = $ _____

c) $(c^4)^4 = $ _____

10 Tommy thinks $(5a^3)^3 = 15a^9$

Explain why Tommy is wrong.

_____

_____

11 Find the difference between the values of $2x^3$ and $(2x)^3$ when

a) $x = 3$

b) $x = -3$

difference = ___

difference = ___

12 Are these sequences linear or not? Justify your answers.

A: t^3 t^6 t^9 t^{12} ...

B: $4p^3$ $7p^3$ $10p^3$ $13p^3$ ...

_____

_____

_____

How did you find these questions?

Very easy   1   2   3   4   5   6   7   8   9   10   Very difficult

122

Revision of handling data

Date:

Let's remember

1 Work out the 10th term of a sequence that is given by the rule $4n + 3$

2 Describe the inequality $x \geq -2$ in words.

_____

3 There is a 16% chance of rain. What is the probability it does not rain?

_____

4 Label the hypotenuse on the triangle.

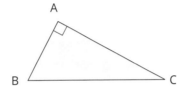

Let's practise

1 The vertical line chart shows the number of attempts some people took to remember their password for a website.

a) How many people remembered their password on the second attempt?

b) How many people are represented altogether?

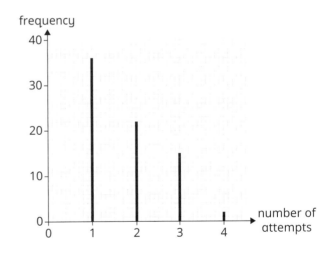

2 In a competition, Huan jumped the following distances in the long jump.

4.23 m   4.16 m   4.3 m   4.21 m   4.16 m   4.41 m

a) Work out the range of the distances Huan jumped. [　　　　] m

b) Find the mean, median and mode of the distances that Huan jumped.

mean = [　　　　] m   median = [　　　　] m   mode = [　　　　] m

3   The frequency diagram shows the times taken by 70 people to complete a crossword puzzle.

a) Write the modal class of the times taken.

_____

b) How many people completed the puzzle in less than 20 minutes?

[   ]

c) Ron says the longest time taken to complete the puzzle was 50 minutes.
Comment on Ron's claim.

_____

_____

4   A Year 9 football team played 24 games in one season.

The results are recorded as win (W), draw (D) or lose (L).

D   W   W   D   W   L   D   D   L   L   W   D

W   L   D   W   L   W   D   D   W   D   W   L

The team is awarded 3 points for every win and 1 point for every draw.

Work out the mean number of points that the team scored over the season.

mean = [   ]

5   Nijah's homework is always marked out of 10

Her last three marks for homework have a median of 8, a range of 3 and a mode of 8

Work out Nijah's marks for her last three homeworks.

_____

6   150 students were asked if they thought their school uniform should be redesigned.

The results are shown in the pie chart.

Work out the number of students who gave each answer.

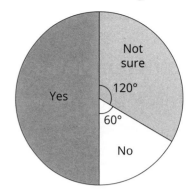

Yes = [   ]   Not sure = [   ]   No = [   ]

7   The table shows the shoe sizes of 20 people. Work out the mean of the shoe sizes.

Shoe size	38	39	40	41
Number of people	2	11	4	3

mean = [   ]

8   The table shows the rainfall in a village over a 10-day period.

Daily rainfall, r mm	$3 < r \leq 4$	$4 < r \leq 5$	$5 < r \leq 6$	$6 < r \leq 7$
Number of days	2	5	0	3

a) Work out an estimate for the mean rainfall over the 10 days.

mean ≈ [   ] mm

b) In which class interval is the median rainfall for the 10 days? _____

9   The mean temperature of a city over a 12-month period is 5°C.

The typical temperature in August, is 16°C.

Work out the mean temperature if August is not included.

mean = [   ] °C

How did you find these questions?

Very easy   1   2   3   4   5   6   7   8   9   10   Very difficult

Mixed Year 9 revision

Date:

Let's remember

1. A pie chart represents 400 people. What angle on the pie chart represents 100 people?

   angle = ▭ °

2. Expand and simplify $(y - 5)(y - 4)$

   _____

3. A fair coin is thrown twice.

   List all the possible outcomes.

   _____

4. Work out the value of a

   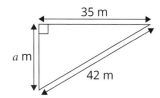

   $a =$ ▭ m

Let's practise

1. Which of the following equations will have straight line graphs?

   Circle your answers. $y = 2x + 3$ $y = x^2 + 3$ $y = \dfrac{2}{x} + 3$ $y = \dfrac{x}{2} + 3$

2. Solve $6x - 2 = 3x + 19$

   $x =$ ▭

3. Decide if the conjectures are true or false.

   a) All the factors of 15 are odd. _____

   b) The squares of prime numbers have exactly three factors. _____

   c) If x is even, x has an even number of factors. _____

4   Angle g is 32° greater than angle h.

Work out the sizes of angles g and h

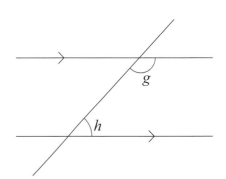

$g =$ [   ] °

$h =$ [   ] °

5   Describe the single transformation that maps shape A to shape B.

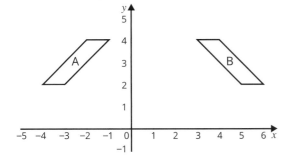

_____

_____

6   Work out the perimeter of quadrilateral ABCD.

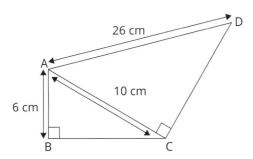

Diagram not drawn to scale

perimeter = [   ] cm

7   When a biased coin is thrown twice, the probability of landing on heads
both times is 0.36

What is the probability that the coin lands on tails both times?

probability = _____

How did you find these questions?

Very easy   1   2   3   4   5   6   7   8   9   10   Very difficult

127

Summer term   Self-assessment

Time to reflect

Look back through the work you have done this term. Think about what you enjoyed and what you found easy or hard. Talk about this to your teacher and someone at home.

Try these questions	How do you feel about this topic? Tick the box.
These two kites are similar. Find the value of x 3 cm 6 cm x 10 cm $x = $ ☐ cm If you need a reminder, look back at enlargement and similarity on pages 89–94	☐ I am confident and could teach someone else. ☐ I think I understand but I need practice. ☐ I don't understand and need help.
The graphs show water flowing into four tanks. Tick the graph that shows water flowing at an increasing rate. A B C D Depth of water / Time If you need a reminder, look back at rates on pages 103–108	☐ I am confident and could teach someone else. ☐ I think I understand but I need practice. ☐ I don't understand and need help
The Venn diagram shows some information about the subjects studied by 50 students in a sixth-form college. English Drama 14 12 5 19 Find the probability that a randomly chosen student studies Drama but not English. _____ If you need a reminder, look back at probability on pages 110–115	☐ I am confident and could teach someone else. ☐ I think I understand but I need practice. ☐ I don't understand and need help.